Why Sink When You Can Swim?

Why Sink When You Can Swim?

by june miller

ZONDERVAN PUBLISHING HOUSE
OF THE ZONDERVAN CORPORATION
GRAND RAPIDS, MICHIGAN 49506

All undesignated Scripture is from the *Revised Standard Version* and is used by permission of the Division of Christian Education of the National Council of the Churches of Christ in the United States of America.
The following have been used by permission:
The Living Bible © 1971 by Tyndale House Publishers, Wheaton, Illinois.
The New Testament in Modern English (Phillips) © 1958, 1959, 1960 by J. B. Phillips.

Library of Congress Catalog Card Number: 73-13057

Printed in the United States of America

These pages are my love-gift to our Lord and Savior Jesus Christ and a way of expressing my gratitude for the tremendous husband with whom I have shared thirty-one years of marriage.

All of the happenings are true events through which God has brought me to discover that my longings for peace, love, and happiness are to be found in the specific principles He has designed for just that purpose.

Today I shall pray for you, as a person whom God loves, that happiness may begin unfolding just a page away.

CONTENTS

PREFACE

If complete happiness could be developed and distributed in seven tiny packages, how many would you take?

God has designed an amazing gift package that is unconditionally guaranteed, when opened and used, to produce peace, freedom from fear, and confident happiness in any life. This package contains seven principles. These are not limited by health, wealth, time, people, places, circumstances, or things, but few of us ever discover more than one of them!

Fourteen-year-old Kevin asked, "What is wrong with our family? It seems as if we are trying to prevent one another from being happy. We pray and go to church, but something is wrong."

Many Christians have become aware of the first principle that has to do with our eternal needs, but have never discovered the bright, sparkling life of adventure which is governed and guided by the remaining six guidelines. These are People Principles and are to direct our living relationships with one another. They hold the secret to a peaceful mind and a happy heart — a heart that transforms a home and the people who live there.

These principles are stepping stones, edged with gold, leading upward to the marvelous treasure available to every person. The most bitter, destructive, and lonely experiences become priceless wealth as we discover the reasons and results that God had in mind. Certainly, choice gifts are often tied with dark ribbons. The greatest jewels are usually displayed against the blackest velvet, and so it is with many of life's events.

As you explore these seven guidelines, may God use this little book to open the wrappings of His priceless love-gifts to you, that your home and your circle of influence may experience their reality in daily living.

Why Sink When You Can Swim?

Hope, the magic nerve of faith
that springs alive in time of crisis,
the golden resilient thread
that leads to the discovery
of God's plan and purpose.

1

Step Forward to Hope

If ever a woman needed hope, I certainly did!

The sharp ringing of the phone broke the calm of the glorious autumn morning. When I answered it, our family doctor said, "June, the results are back from yesterday's biopsy. You have cancer. I'll meet you at the hospital in about thirty minutes."

Thirty minutes! I had thirty minutes to prepare myself and my family for cancer surgery. My thoughts raced through our family experiences. There had been several cases of malignancy, including two of my brothers. Each case had been terminal.

I clutched the phone. "Dr. Brown, who will be doing the surgery?"

"Well, it's Saturday and almost noon. It's pretty hard to get a surgeon this late in the weekend, but we'll get someone. See you in thirty minutes."

Certainly there was no reassurance in that remark. It sounded as if I might end up with the services of a veterinarian!

Minutes later I walked through the bedrooms of our five children and committed each life into Christ's hands. Dear, tiny Jeff was just three years old. Joy was a beautiful little girl who seemed so fragile among her four brothers. Thirteen-year-old Mike with his love for people and abundance of friends would find satisfying attachments to fill any sense of loss. Perhaps Mark's music would be his stabilizer. Ray would soon be twenty-one. . . .

Why had God chosen such difficult timing? Would I come home to my dear family again?

It was not inconceivable to me that God could supply the children with a better mother or that He could have in reserve a wife far superior to myself. For God had taught me one thing well: He never removes anything unless He has something far better to give in its place! And certainly if this was to be the time God had chosen to move me on to the home He had prepared for eternity, I did not need to be afraid.

But in a moment of crisis fear is not the only emotion involved. None of us are eager to be replaced or displaced, and even though there could be a better mother or wife available for my family, I was not willing to step aside, especially to the possibility of a terminal illness.

There were the endless needs of the family to be considered. Without insurance and with a limited income, money would be a problem. We had no relatives nearby to care for the children, the cooking, the laundry, and other daily details.

But God is always on the job!

Like a gentle whisper, the Holy Spirit spoke to my heart: "Present your (body) as a living sacrifice, holy and acceptable to God, which is your spiritual worship" (Romans 12:1).

How strange that this verse should be so vivid to me at a time like this. Hadn't I given my body to God years ago? Hadn't He used it to reach many people with the story of His love? He knew that I loved Him....

Yes, but I needed to be reminded that my body was no longer mine. How quickly I had claimed responsibility for that which I had given God, simply because something had gone wrong. I was ready to step in and take over, as though I doubted God was on the job. For that is what worry is: Trying to do God's job for Him. It is taking upon ourselves the responsibility that He has reserved for Himself alone. If I had given my body to Him, then it was not my body that had cancer, but His — for I was His. Could He not take care of that which was His? If not, why should I presume that I could?

I committed that moment to God.

"Father, help me to look beyond the events of this moment and to know that because You love me, You will help me discover a deeper faith, a brighter hope than I have ever known."

Arriving at the hospital a few minutes later, I was met by a doctor whom I did not know. He introduced himself as a "Mayo cancer specialist." After a quick stop in the x-ray department, we walked down a long corridor. Pushing open the double doors that led to Surgery, the doctor said, "June, we have both lived in Chicago, and I wonder if you may have met a friend whom I came to know while living there?"

When I asked who his friend was, he replied, "Jesus Christ," and proceeded to share the joy and reality he had found in the living, loving Savior who had guided his life each day since that time.

When we walked into the brightly lighted operating room, he introduced me to the three doctors who would assist with the surgery. Each of them shared just as eagerly the genuineness of belonging to God's family.

In the calendar of men it was a Saturday afternoon when doctors were just not available in the bright vacationland of San Diego. Yet in God's timing it was a unique day. It was a day in which He had reserved the finest cancer specialists available in that part of the country. And they were all men who were committed to Jesus Christ. It was a day when I received one of the most precious love-gifts that God has ever given me. Dark ribbons? Yes, but many valuable gifts are packaged that way.

"June, before we administer anesthetic, may we pray together?" asked the doctor.

What a setting for an old-fashioned miracle! A room filled with glaring lights, complex equipment, and a team of specialists reserved to meet the needs of a simple wife and mother. But most of all, there was God.

"Father, I give You my hands and I give You June's body. Will You work through me as the Great Physician and remove all diseased tissue that she may have perfect health? Thank You, Father."

Before I came to the hospital, God had reminded me that I had given Him my body. Now this doctor was reaffirming my commitment. No one can give another person to God, but we can commit them to His care. Each person has the privilege of relinquishing himself into the hands of the Savior. I am the only person who can positively present my life to God for His use and direction, and the same is true for you.

It has been seven years since that significant autumn day, and much has happened during that time. The cancer surgery was successful, but there was still the matter of the scar to face. I had been told that women who experience a radical mastectomy usually undergo emotional adjustment problems. In the beginning the scar was red and angry, and there was a lingering physical tenderness.

Now, seven years later, the diseased tissue is gone, and I have marvelous health. All that is left is a faded scar, but a scar that is a treasure in disguise. It is a constant reminder of the *hope* God gave me through that experience.

I had always been afraid of fear. Not so much a fear of cancer, although our family had had many experiences with it, but a terrifying buried fear that could creep up in times of crisis. A wild, desperate, consuming fear of encountering an event that I would not be able to cope with — a fear of knowing real panic.

In facing this cancer surgery, I found that God removed forever my fear that I would be unable to walk through a great crisis. Along with the cancer tissue, God had removed the diseased tissue of emotional attitudes — guilts, fears, and failures — so that I might truly be free and happy.

My scar is also a reminder of the marvelous goodness of our God in keeping us together as a family. Since facing the possible loss of each other, Hal and I have a deeper, richer love for each other and for our children. The children, in turn, have learned to value and appreciate us more than ever.

Finally, my scar is a unique glory to share with other women who have desperate fears — women who need to know the healing power of God. In the same way, that very thing which may seem such a limitation to you can become your emblem of uniqueness, your story for His glory. Focus your eyes upon the beauty of Jesus and His adequacy and thank Him — yes, praise Him — for your scar. As it becomes your living memorial of His love in keeping you each day, you will be used of God to brighten the life of someone who is in the darkness of fear and without hope.

Now, I realize that some of you are a step ahead of me, asking, "But what about physical limitations which cannot be cured by surgery or medicine? What about those things in our lives which we cannot change?"

Lou is a friend of mine who has a physical limitation which prevents her from going out among people. So she has given her phone as a love-gift to God. She is constantly sharing encouragement from the Bible and praying by phone with those who have needs. Lou told me recently that about a hundred people had "just dropped in" during the past Christmas season to show their appreciation for her investment of love during the year. I wonder how many of them would have bothered if those same hours had been spent in focusing upon her limitations?

Each of us has exactly 1,440 minutes a day. We have 10,080 minutes a week and approximately 524,160 minutes a year. We are responsible for what we do with them. They are a treasure which we can only spend once. Nor do we know when we will have used the last one in God's appointed time bank. God has given us minutes, hours, days, and possibly years to invest for our future happiness and His present delight. Time is valuable, but it is limited to this world system. Our abilities increase with use, and the results will go on forever.

Take a New Look at Yourself

But it is you, yourself, whom God dearly loves and values. He does not love you for your performance, although it may be worthwhile. He does not love you because you are capable of doing certain things. He does not love you for your possessions, your contacts, or even your influence. He does not love you because your features are flawless or your personality enchanting.

He loves you because He has created you!

Before your birth, God had the ability, love, and wisdom to design you with such exacting care that you might have the very talents, abilities, and other essentials to fulfill His desire for your future. How important it is, then, that you discover what His plans are and become interested in those things which interest Him.

God has designed the human body so that it is limited to time and earth life. It is subject to the natural laws by which God maintains our planet and is wonderfully designed for contact with the earth, its people, places, and things. But the body is also to be a container which the Spirit of God can enter and live in so that He might be known through our lives.

"Do you not know that you are God's temple (or home) and that God's Spirit dwells (lives) in you?... Do you not know that your body is a temple of the Holy Spirit within you, which you have from God? You are not your own; you were bought with a price. So glorify God in your body. . . . For we are the temple of the living God; as God said, 'I will live in them and move among them, and I will be their God, and they shall be my people' " (1 Corinthians 3:16; 6:19; 2 Corinthians 6:16).

Regardless of the imperfections we may have, God has designed our body as the place in which He finds pleasure in living. In Revelation 3:20 we learn that He enters our body by invitation only, for He says, ". . . if any one hears my voice and opens the door, I will come in. . . ." Just as we open the door to a friend who knocks, so we can open the door of our life and heart and invite Jesus Christ to come in and share the body that He has given us. He inhabits our body through the Holy Spirit as we invite Him to do so. From that moment our body becomes the house in which He lives, and we will never be alone; He is always with us. He walks in our shoes, lives in our lives, loves through us, and uses each of us in a unique way.

In spite of this uniqueness, however, most of us at one time or another have longed to trade places with someone else. At least I certainly have.

Several years ago I discovered that God really loved me, although I could not imagine why. Seemingly, I had nothing to offer but a lot of fears and guilts which I was more than happy to relinquish. During that time I longed to have someone with whom I could learn to pray. Then I met a lovely woman who became my spiritual friend. She was charming, talented, and a delight to everyone who knew her. Week by week I watched the beautiful harmony of her relationship with her pastor husband. I thought she lived in a world of perfection and happiness.

"Oh, if I could learn all the wonderful things of God this family seems to know," I thought. "If I could just be like that lovely lady — or, better still, trade places with her, if only for a day!"

Then came the news that my friend had been rushed to a large downtown hospital, desperately ill with polio, and was at first pronounced dead on arrival. Through the miracle of prayer and surgery she was restored to her family, but how glad I was that the same God who permitted her to go through such an experience had seen fit to protect me from the disease to which we had both been exposed. My Lord knew that neither I nor my family was ready yet for such a test.

God's purpose for each life is distinctly different. There is absolutely no other person in this world who can fulfill the purpose for which God has designed you.

Experts in the field of ecology are just discovering the damage that is being done to the balance of nature as certain species are becoming extinct. If all the birds were removed from the earth, it soon would be overrun by crop-destroying and germ-carrying insects and rodents. Nothing else can fulfill the role assigned to birds. It is their purpose in creation.

But how foolish it would be for a bird to try to play the role of a star or a planet. It could not survive the vast expanse of space without atmosphere nor maintain the necessary orbit. Nor could the planet or star rid a flower bed of insects.

Why is it that we recognize the rightness of nature operating by God's design and purpose and still fail to have a confident trust in God's character of love and wisdom to direct our lives?

He is capable of planning and completing something wonderful in our future. We can look forward with *hope* to that plan. ". . . hope that is seen is not hope. For who hopes for what he sees? But if we hope for what we do not see, we wait for it with patience" (Romans 8:24, 25).

I cannot see the future events of my life, but each happening can become an exciting adventure — even a routine shopping day.

It was that kind of a routine day on which I found a lovely pair of shoes on sale. Eagerly I tried them on, but to my disappointment they were only a size five. They certainly could not fit my size-seven foot. Returning them to the shelf, I felt cheated that they would not meet my need, although I would never have had a moment of "happy feet" in those shoes that did not fit the pattern.

Turning away that day I said, "Lord, I thank You

for whatever provision You have for my need of shoes." Passing between the rows of boxes, I moved toward the door. Then I saw the most beautiful shoes I had ever seen, and they were reduced from fifty dollars to fifteen. Slipping my foot into them, I almost squealed with delight at the sheer comfort and beauty. Those shoes have given me three years of marvelous service, for they were designed for a foot like mine.

How often do we try to cram a size-seven life into a seemingly attractive five? There are marvelous things ahead when a person walks willingly, expectantly, one day at a time in the path that God sets before her. Being faithful in the little things of today opens tomorrow's door to a wider and more exciting vista. I am learning not to expect God to reveal His ultimate purpose for me while I am still in the kindergarten of experience. He does not let us skip over any steps! He is not finished with my life yet. He is not finished with yours.

However, if you would like to speed up the process of becoming a lovelier you, here are three steps that will help.

(1) *Take an inventory of your good qualities.*

Stand before your mirror and take a good look at yourself. What do you see? If you had the privilege of changing anything about your physical appearance, what would you do? Add an inch of height or take one away? Trade blue eyes for brown, blonde hair for black? Straighten a nose or slim down a chin? I do not believe there is any person in this world, beauty queens included, who would not want to make some alteration.

There are some things that can be changed simply by good grooming, adequate rest and exercise, and the best choice of foods. But bone structure, natural coloring, and many other physical details cannot be changed without radical or cosmetic surgery. Some things can never be changed.

For the moment, disregard the features you do not like and concentrate on the others. Eyes, brows, hair, teeth, dimples, skin, fingers — there are some really good features, aren't there? A new hair style or a different application of make-up can emphasize good features and minimize those less pleasing.

For example, I used to detest the contour of my forehead. Now it has become the motivation to develop nice hair styles. As a teen-ager I disliked my mouth; I felt it was much too large. But I have learned that a warm, happy smile will use it to far better advantage than a discouraging droop!

I'm sure God had a sense of humor when He put us together, but He also had wisdom and tender compassion. He had a reason for everything He did, and that brings us to the second step.

(2) *Look at yourself from God's point of view.*

One day I realized that my God was not a remote, uncaring God somewhere in the sky. He was alive, real, and right there with me. I told Him how I felt about myself.

"Father, I do not like many things about myself, including the mouth and forehead You have designed. But because I know You are a God of wisdom and love, You must have had a reason for making them exactly like You have. I am sorry that I have criticized and despised Your handiwork, and if You value me this way, then I shall, too. I want to give You the full use of my mouth and my head, that You might be able to accomplish the purpose for which You prepared them. Forgive me for forgetting that my body belongs to You and not to me. I thank You, too, that You have a new flawless body ready for me when you have finished using this one here on earth and I can come to live in Your home.

"Lord, there's one more thing. Thank You for living in my body the way it is. I want You to have the freedom to make any changes that You know are best."

Tell Jesus how you feel about yourself right now.

(3) *Expect good things to happen in your life.*

After my chat with God, I took my Bible and wrote the date and the happening.

"Given to You: one mouth and one head, that You might fill both with Yourself and Your truth. Dated: July 19, 1960."

There are times when I am tempted to go back to the old attitudes, especially when weary, ill, or discouraged, and this has been a reminder of my agreement with God. The me I see is not the finished product.

Not only am I changing, but the events in my life are changing too. There is a new expectancy, a buoyant hope alive and growing. There is just a tiny glimmer of God's long-range plan for me. My memo has served as a spotlight, reminding me to search for *the positive use of my life in every negative situation.*

Something good *is* coming your way, too. It is God's purpose for you! If for the moment you seem to be shrouded in black velvet, it is because you are His treasured jewel — His original masterpiece.

> "*Beloved, we are God's children now; it does not yet appear what we shall be, but we know that when he appears we shall be like him, for we shall see him as he is. And every one who thus hopes in him purifies himself as he is pure*" (1 John 3:2, 3).

There can be no shadows
without the presence of the sun.
The shadows of fear often mark
the path that leads us to discover
the freedom of life in the Son.

2

Step Up to Freedom

Do you ever feel as if God has padlocked the heavens? Does He seem to be on a permanent vacation — at least as far as you are concerned?

I have wondered at times: "What *is* God doing? Where is He?" However, at that point my real search was not for God, but for a way out of my own attitudes which had erected the gate that was shutting Him out of an area of my life.

Walking along the California coast one day, I watched the pounding breakers that were like an echo of my anxieties. Then, as if carried by the sea breeze, God's voice spoke to me through my thoughts.

"You should not be afraid and disturbed by secret doubts, June. I am with you. I will never leave you nor desert you. Because I love you, I have carefully designed the events you need to produce the beauty that is not yet revealed in your life.

"I am designing and controlling the happenings, the places, and the people that you come in contact with so I may cut you loose from those things which cause you fear. Don't look at those situations so constantly. Look at me and remember that I love you and that you *need* this experience. You are going to become free of every destructive emotion — free of worry, fear, guilt, and the feelings of inadequacy, for I am adequate and I live within you.

"You are to learn from each experience. Don't depend on any person, place, or thing as your security, for it will only slow down the development of your character. It will take extra lessons to set you free then, for those very people and things upon which you would like to lean are limited. They are going through constant change just as you are.

"I am your only security; I do not change. The hurts, disappointments, and disillusionments that you have endured in the past can become the basis for the greatest happiness and beauty in the future. There is no hurry. I have all the time in the world and then eternity! Relax in My arms, for I love you. I have come to set you free, and you will be free indeed!"

My thoughts were interrupted by the deep fog-horns announcing a change in weather conditions in the channel. How quickly the walls of gray fog had rolled in, blotting out the sun. Sky, land, and sea seemed to wear a shroud of impenetrable gray; trees, flowers and neighbors had disappeared. I felt strangely depressed and lonely.

But even as I watched, the winds that had brought the fog in from the sea carried it on to the valley. Soon it had all passed and the sun was shining. Birds were singing and the sky and water seemed a more dazzling blue. The fragrance of the flowers was sweeter than ever.

Sun, sea, sky, and land had remained unchanged. Only my view of them had been affected. Because of the passing cloud, my appreciation for the beauty of the place had been enriched. Things that I had taken for granted were now enjoyed. The chill gray clouds of illness, financial loss, conflict, and misun-derstandings with life partners, children, and friends are the gold-lined clouds through which God will reveal His Son. There can be no shadows without the presence of the sun.

Residents in certain areas of California boast that the sun shines every day. Seldom is a rain cloud seen in the sky. But that land is a desert! All sunshine makes a desert, and God does not intend that our life should become a desert.

"You shall be like a watered garden, like a spring of water, whose waters fail not. . . . Then shall your light break forth like the dawn, and your healing shall spring up speedily. . . . Instead of the thorn shall come up the cypress; instead of the brier shall come up the myrtle. . . . For you shall go out in joy, and be led forth in peace" (Isaiah 58:11, 8; 55:13, 12). These words were spoken hundreds of years ago to the people of God, the Hebrew nation, yet they are a promise to all who are His people today. They speak of that which God delights in doing in the lives of those who love Him.

Fred Beard of Eugene, Oregon, once said, "God holds His child near His heart and in the hollow of His hand. Then He covers him with the other. Nothing can touch that child except those things designed by Him. He opens His fingers wide enough to let in the events that are necessary to develop that special bit of character that God knows His child needs."

Freedom From Limiting Fears

Does your heart whisper, "Why did God 'open His fingers wide enough' to let in this particular problem"? Marion discovered the answer to this when she had to stand in an Oregon court with her nineteen-year-old son and face his involvement in drugs.

"I died a thousand deaths," Marion says. "Our

hearts were broken. We were terribly concerned for Tom's future, and there was the added agony of awareness that we were a point of gossip as a family. But it has thrown us back into the arms of God as our only security. We have given Him our reputation as parents. We have learned that we are not immune to the problems other parents face. We are no longer exalted, untouched, maintaining a facade of success. The superior wisdom that once tinged our discussion of the difficulties of others has melted into a deep desire to understand parents and youth.

"Tom is learning the genuiness of love that does not condemn. Through his own experience his life is being reclaimed, and he is working with other young people who have desperate needs. We are becoming open to one another, and there is marvelous freedom from the attempt to protect our image. In facing the possibility of being rejected by others, we have become free of the fear of it."

Freedom is a result of confrontation. It becomes a reality as we face those issues that limit our lives with fears, anxieties, and frustrations. It is in the darkness of night that we appreciate the light of a lamp. We never need it in the sunshine!

It is when frightening experiences must be met that we draw on hidden courage. The law of growth is use, and the muscles of faith are developed in the exercise of reaching out for solutions — in climbing to new levels of maturity.

This became a literal experience for me. I was terribly afraid of heights and had thought that flying would terrify me. But one day an emergency arose, and I knew I had to take a plane to San Francisco. I had to fly to meet the needs of someone who was more important to me than my fear. As the plane rose into the air, I looked down on the receding homes, lakes, and mountains and my heart seemed to leap with joy. I found myself humming, "I'm going higher, yes, higher each day." The prison of fear had been thrown open. Why had I avoided such fantastic beauty that could be enjoyed only from this elevation? My pulse raced and I thought, "Oh, the glory of the throne room of God! It will far exceed our wildest fantasies if He has designed such magnificence as this. If I could just rise higher until I see Him!" *I had been set free!*

How kind of God to arrange this opportunity as a stepping stone to freedom. Since then I have enjoyed countless flights, some in tiny two-passenger planes, flying into remote areas in Saskatchewan and island territories in the Pacific to share with women who need to know Jesus.

Jesus said, "I came that they may have life, and have it abundantly" (John 10:10). The "abundant life" becomes increasingly free of anxiety, apprehension, and worry. Guilt, failure, resentment, and bitterness can be removed. Through the honest recognition and release of issues and persons into Christ's hands, we can begin moving toward this experience. That which we dread may be the happening we need to discover the reality of an abundant or overflowing life — a life free of limiting fears.

Freedom From False Security

Each of our lives has different circumstances that express the same basic need. Strangly enough, it was seeming financial tragedy that brought increased security and happiness for Jeri. It had been difficult to assume the role of both father and mother to her two daughters. Long hours at work that was physically exhausting added to the stress, and day-care for the girls had become increasingly expensive and inadequate.

Then suddenly her job was terminated without notice. The loss of all income, followed by a week of fruitless job-hunting, resulted in near panic.

She sobbed, "I can't take care of my family any longer."

We talked together about her needs, and then I asked, "Jeri, are you willing to ask and trust God to do for you what you cannot do yourself? Remember, He loves you and the children He has given to you."

After putting those needs in our Lord's hands, Jeri began watching expectantly for God's answer to her faith. Then the call came to manage an apartment building. She was provided with a lovely, convenient apartment, an income, and the chance to be at home with her little daughters. That which seemed disastrous actually released her from the false security of an inadequate job and led her to discover the freedom of becoming an independent person under God's loving headship.

It is His desire to give us the best, but in order to do so, it usually involves a cutting loose from that on which we have depended and leaned. God is not so limited that He must supply through any one job. His resources are vast and creative, filled with unimaginable variety. We fear the loss of material things that represent security to us. Only as we are severed from them do we discover the unchanging security and adventure of receiving from the hand of God that which He has already reserved and made available for us. We learn this lesson individually, but there is a striking example of it in God's dealings with an entire nation in Old Testament days.

Hundreds of years ago God's people were held in slavery by a foreign political power. Then a man named Moses took God at His word and believed His promise that if those people would show confidence in their God while they were in bondage, they would be brought into a marvelous land of freedom and provision. They followed the directions God had given them, and an entire nation began a night march. As they approached the Red Sea, they heard the thundering hoofs of the enemy's army overtaking them. They looked ahead at the Red Sea and were terrified. They looked behind and thought they were doomed.

But God had designed the very experience they needed to find security that the greatest army could never shatter! How could they ever forget the day the living God parted the waters of that sea to make a path for them. Yet the very path they walked safely became the grave of the enemy as the waters closed over them.

There had to be a Red Sea to show the mighty love, provision, and power of God for His people and to show the inadequacy of the enemy's cleverest plans and greatest strength. It was there that the enemy was defeated. It was in the crossing of the Red Sea that God's people found their freedom.

Freedom From Circumstances

Our conflicts and encounters are custom-made by God to draw us closer to Him. Consider the woman in the New Testament who found her life style, with all its guilts, prejudices, and confused religious ideas, changed in a few minutes as a result of a meeting by God.

It was while the Samaritan woman was doing an ordinary, dull, routine job — drawing water from the village well — that she encountered none other than Jesus Christ, the Messiah, in the garb of a weary traveler (John 4). When He asked her for a drink of water, her entire concern was that a member of the Jewish race should ask her, a despised Samaritan, for a drink and the fact that He had no utensil with which to draw the water.

Her attention was focused on circumstances and limitations, while Christ wanted her to discover His unlimited provision for her needs — needs that she was not, as yet, willing to discuss. Neither the limitation of who we are, what we are, or where we are, hinders God's tremendous purpose for us. We must catch the right glimpse of *Who* He is, *What* He is, and *Where* He is. The God who put the water in the well is not limited by the lack of a bucket!

What exciting things happen when we exchange our self-centered view, our "I-land," for the outward and upward Christ-centered view.

I'm sure the Samaritan woman never dreamed that anyone could meet God by a hot, dusty well while doing a routine task. Were there not strict rules and rituals to be observed in meeting God? But Jesus meets all people where they are, deep in their needs. He reveals Himself as God over all circumstances, but most clearly when we are willing to relinquish the preoccupation with self. We must put down the "water-pot" of self-dependence to have our hands available to receive that which He has come to offer.

When the woman simply believed, she met Jesus, the Savior. Quickly she dashed into the town to tell others that she had found the One who had set her free from people, places, and circumstances. Her hands were emptied of the water jugs and her heart was emptied of its guilt and shame. Both were left at His dear feet.

What a transformation those people must have seen in the face and attitude of this woman who, in a moment of time, had seen the reality of God's love, forgiveness, and cleansing.

God is arranging the circumstances in each of our lives so that we might face the issues that cause us fear, anxiety, guilt, loneliness, and separation from others. He does it because He wants us to be free. "You will know the truth, and the truth will make you free" (John 8:32).

For many people one of the most traumatic of the freeing experiences is a major geographical move — especially if there seems to be no security to look forward to in the new area.

"Would you rather live in Seattle, Miami, or New York?" the voice across the table asked. A voice that twenty-two years of marriage had taught me was apt to bring many surprises. My husband Hal is a man of keen intellect, generous heart, and restless, adventurous spirit. That spirit led us across twenty-eight states in our first two years of marriage. The following years had included the rest of the states plus Canada and Mexico. Life had never been very secure, but it certainly hadn't been dull!

Still, I really wasn't prepared for this question. Why would anyone move across the United States with no definite job in mind? Not even a single friend or contact?

So many uncertainties would have to be faced. Where would we live: a house or an apartment? What about the cost of living? Schools for the children? If the climate were different, appropriate clothing would be needed. What kind of church would we find? Would people accept us?

My eyes filled with tears at the prospect of leaving all those things that represented security. Happy experiences, dear friends — those who had cared for our family in such a marvelous way during illness and surgery. How could we possibly trade these dear people and rich friendships in on unknowns? The thought of breaking loose from all that had been our home seemed unbearable. There didn't seem to be anything to which to cling. The old security blanket was getting quite a tug, yet Hal seemed sure that God intended us to go. After much discussion, Seattle was chosen as our new home.

Freedom From Fear of Failure

The first year in the new area was rough. Absolutely nothing seemed to go right. Even the furniture deliveries were wrong. A queen-size box spring arrived with a regular-size mattress. A discount furniture store uncrated a red and yellow dinette set instead of the blue and green that we had ordered. Sometimes I laughed through my tears at the seeming comedy of errors that our life had become. Sometimes a quick little S.O.S. had to go winging its way to God's throne to prevent the "I told you so" feeling that fought for utterance.

God is not in the business of making failures; yet everything about us seemed to be failing. We watched as our business investment failed and we had to sacrifice our lovely new home. Next, the new car went, and finally even the furniture had to be sold to meet current living expenses.

Yet as the pressures became greater, God became more real. It was as if His Presence flooded all the corners of the house as it was emptied of things.

Then came the almost desperate job-hunting trip. During Hal's absence, a friend picked us up for church. For some strange reason she made a wrong turn and we found ourselves on the cliff above Puget Sound.

The view was breath-taking and I whispered, "What if God gives us a place over here!"

Emma's funny little laugh echoed as she said, "If you're going to dream, dream first class."

Yet just a week later, God led Hal to a new job and gave us possession of a lovely brick home in that very block.

Another eleven months elapsed before the court for the disposition of the estate had acted in our favor and accepted our offer to purchase the home. That year provided the time for us to accumulate the funds for a down payment. Who would ever have dreamed that God would give us a home with such a magnificent view of Mt. Rainier and the Sound. How wonderfully kind He had been in releasing us from the first house where there had been no view and a thirty-year contract.

Seemingly it had been a year of total loss. But those seeming failures were actually an emptying process essential to greater success. In a vineyard, the dead limbs that have borne the summer grapes must be cut away before the new growth can begin. This same process is at the heart of God's training program. He controls the circumstances, no matter how painful or bitter, and uses them to perform His work in our lives.

The months that followed were exciting, and the last night of that year was unforgettable. As we munched chicken together in a drive-in restaurant, a new Cadillac pulled in beside us.

Looking at it a bit wistfully, Hal said, "Honey, I've always wanted one of those, perhaps as a sign of achievement. Now we can afford it." After a thoughtful pause he continued, "You know, I really can't justify spending that much money on just a set of wheels for our family. I don't think I'll ever buy one until we can support at least two missionaries through our own family efforts. God can use that more than we need a Cadillac."

My heart sang with a grateful, "Thank You for a growing sense of values."

A few days later when the president of Hal's company came out from the East Coast, he walked into Hal's office and handed him a set of keys, an automobile title, and a check to cover transfer of the title of a beautiful new Cadillac convertible, complete with stereo and extras. It was a bonus for Hal's outstanding achievement in his first year with the company!

God does not always have immediate, tangible

gifts like this in our future, but to us it was further proof of His promise in Psalm 37:4: "Take delight in the Lord, and he will give you the desires of your heart."

Yes, that was quite a year. A house with no view exchanged for one with a magnificent view. A Chevrolet for a Cadillac. A mediocre job for satisfying achievement. Relinquishment! Surely it had been well taught. We had learned that the greater the trial or difficulty, the greater the Father's blessing and provision, although not always in a material way. Truly, God is no man's debtor. He always gives far more than He receives.

The place of relinquishment does not come on the mountaintop, but in the deepest and bleakest of valleys in confrontation with those things we dread and fear most. At that moment, when we are cut loose from all that is comfortable, pleasant, and secure — even our loved ones — we finally realize that we have only God. Gay wrappings of life are torn away and we begin to see Him as He is and find confidence in nothing short of His character and love for us. Then, at last, He is free to give us that which His heart longs to give: our best happiness and a peace that is not dependent on things temporary.

"For from him and through him and to him are all things. To him be glory for ever. . . . Do not be conformed to this world but be transformed by the renewal of your mind, that you may prove what is the will of God, what is good and acceptable and perfect" (Romans 11:36; 12:2).

Freedom From Materialism

To be "conformed to this world" is such a continual temptation. The fear of having absolutely nothing and no one upon whom I can depend has loomed large in my life. My need for identification with people, places, and things is natural, but I need to remember that nothing is really mine. It is all on loan to me so that I may learn to use it to the best advantage.

Jesus said, "Don't store up treasures here on earth where they can erode away or may be stolen. Store them in heaven where they will never lose their value, and are safe from thieves. . . . Don't worry about *things* — food, drink, and clothes. For you already have life and a body — and they are far more important than what to eat and wear. Look at the birds! They don't worry about what to eat — they don't need to sow or reap or store up food — for your heavenly Father feeds them. And you are far more valuable to him than they are. Will all your worries add a single moment to your life?

"And why worry about your clothes! Look at the field lilies! They don't worry about theirs. Yet King Solomon in all his glory was not clothed as beautifully as they . . . your heavenly Father already knows perfectly well that you need them (food and clothing), and he will give them to you if you give him first place in your life and live as he wants you to. So don't be anxious about tomorrow. God will take care of your tomorrow too. Live one day at a time" (Matthew 6:19, 20, 25-29, 31-34, *Living Bible*).

These words were spoken by the One who made heaven and earth and you! There wouldn't be a blade of grass on earth or a bird in the sky if He had not put it there, and He did it all without any help!

When I look at the magnificent beauty of the blue waters of Puget Sound, bordered by the snow-capped splendor of the Cascade Mountains on one side and the Olympics on the other, my heart cries out, "Oh, God, what a beautiful world You have made for us, and yet how badly we have treated it." Only the scars are man-made: the power poles with their network of dark wires, the hillsides left bare from early logging days, the jet vapor streaking through the distant pall of a pulp mill.

Yet, if there is still so much beauty in this scarred world, just think what heaven will be like, fresh from the hand of God! The God who paints such magnificent scenes on the canvas of the blue sky against the backdrop of nature is painting a far more marvelous scene through our daily experiences. We aren't quite high enough yet to see them from His perspective. Until we release our worries, anxieties, and fears into His hands we shall never have the freedom of knowing that absolutely nothing can happen to us that is too big for God to handle. If you can trust God to provide for you in eternity, can't you also trust Him to handle the happenings during this short period of time that we call life?

Freedom From Monotony

It is not always the great traumatic event that brings an agony of conflict into our lives. Sometimes it is the daily routine of sameness. The daily cleaning and laundry can seem so monotonous. Yet when we recognize that God is in those mundane moments, they become transformed.

Have you ever considered giving your housework to God? It can be a real revelation.

For example, consider the day you have worked so hard mopping, waxing, and cleaning. Then the three o'clock onslaught hits the door. In troop the kids with muddy shoes, dogs, and friends. School books, lunch boxes, and jackets find their respective corners and the tornado has left its wake of destruction.

Perhaps you still have enough energy and control to calmly reprimand the children and remind them to pick up their assorted belongings, but it could be that the sight of those muddy tracks is just too much. It is then that you need to take a deep breath and remind yourself that if you have given this house to God, it is not *your* floor. While you have used your energy to clean it, His hand has covered yours. He has walked each step with you. This moment of quiet reflection and prayer could save hurt feelings over harsh words spoken in anger.

And then there's the ironing. I had always detested this chore. It seemed such a waste of time. The same clothes were there again next week, if not sooner. But one day I discovered that my ironing board could become the most interesting place in my home. I was ironing a shirt for Hal and thinking, "If I didn't have so much ironing today, I would have a wonderful time with God. I would pray about that important meeting for my husband, the vacation we want to take, the friends who are in the hospital. . . ."

Suddenly I realized that it doesn't take a great deal of imagination or creativity to plow through the ironing. If my mind was free to resent, why wasn't it free to move out and touch lives of people through prayer?

Since that day my ironing board has become my prayer chapel. I now cover the board with bright-flowered covers instead of dull gray, and as I work, I pray. I pray for my grandchildren as they wear the jeans I'm pressing. I pray for a son whose shirt I iron. "Oh, Father, thank You for Jeff. Help him to be honest and fair in sports. Help him to absorb everything that he can that is good in school today so that he may be prepared for the future You have planned for him." Next, a blouse for Joy: "Dear Jesus, when she wears this tonight on a date, help her to include You in every activity. . . ."

But my chapel isn't limited to prayer. The phone is kept on the end of the board. When a friend calls with a need to talk, I flip on the iron and enjoy using the time to share with someone while the work is being done. It's a grand time, too, to memorize Bible passages!

Freedom to Receive and Give Love

I guess the most frustrating thing in my household is that time when everyone seems to fail to perform and I am left holding the bag. It was at a moment like that when I discovered a marvelous truth.

Early that morning a phone call brought the news that we were to have a group of people whom I did not know for dinner. This meant a total change of plans to allow for marketing and cleaning as well as dinner preparation.

After the family had left for the day, I walked into Joy's room. Now Joy never left the house without having made her bed and hung up her clothes. That is, almost never, and today was that "almost" day! Not only were the blankets tumbled on the floor, but it seemed as if all her clothes were too.

I was angry! How could she let me down on a day like this?

Then it hit me: Did I withhold this room when I gave our home to God? Wasn't He in control of this day? What was the lesson He knew I needed to learn from this experience?

Looking at the facts instead of my feelings, I realized first of all that the bed needed to be changed anyway. A few minutes later it occurred to me that it had been some time since I had given Joy's room a good, thorough cleaning rather than the once-over-lightlies. Soon the carpet was vacuumed, the border of floorboard waxed, and the furniture polished.

Then, as a final touch, I placed a rose on a tray of fruit with a little note that read: "Isn't God wonderful to permit us to have such a lovely home? Your room is beautiful . . . it was fun to do. Love you. Mom." I went on to other things, feeling as though I had just moved a mountain.

Later that afternoon the door opened quietly and a dear little girl slipped into the room where she expected to find a disaster area. After a long silence, two arms slipped around my neck as she said, "Mom, I sure appreciate your doing my room. Can I iron for you or help with dinner?"

I thought, "What a wall was torn down by simply showing Christian love to one of my own family." There is something special about using those things that irritate us as a means of showing love — often to the very people who have caused the irritation. Every wall must be torn down before any real love can be exchanged.

Whether it is in the trauma of life-shaking situations or in the endless monotony of everyday living, we find that our life is constantly bringing us face to face with issues that we fear. We can try to hide from them, or we can face them with God. It is only in the confrontation that we learn to live above, not under, the circumstance. It is only in confrontation that we learn the lesson that He has for us. It is only in confrontation that we learn to give and receive gracious forgiveness — not because it is deserved, but because it is the Christian way of life. The putting to death of selfishness is the birthplace of freedom.

Catch sight of Jesus as He truly is and then reveal Him to others, for it is He who said, "The truth will make you free" (John 8:32). It is the truth of what we feel and why, the truth of giving ourselves to one another in love in the way that Jesus Christ gave Himself for us. "I am the way, and the truth, and the life; no one comes to the Father, but by me" (John 14:6).

Truth plus responsible, loving action equals freedom. Your home and heart can be free through your response to Jesus Christ and His commands.

"So if the Son makes you free, you will be free indeed!" (John 8:36).

Security that can be taken away is insecurity. "The skies shall disappear like smoke, and the earth shall wear out like a garment.... But my salvation lasts forever; my righteous rule will never die nor end" (Isaiah 51:6, *Living Bible*).

3

Step Into Security

When you were a young girl did you ever dream of becoming a lovely lady with beautiful clothes, an elegant home, and a charming husband? Perhaps your dreams were peopled with delightful, happy children. But dreams seldom prepare us for the reality of life, nor do they equip us with the knowledge of how to achieve the dream.

Seldom does a young bride anticipate the many roles that lie ahead as she becomes wife and mother. We have intensely specialized training for most jobs and occupations, but there is little preparation for the woman who is to become hostess, secretary, counselor, public relations manager, cultural representative, bookkeeper, administrator, dietician, cook, seamstress, chauffeur, nurse, teacher, laundress, playmate, stand-in for Amy Vanderbilt, referee, spiritual advisor, and dispenser of love and comfort.

But that's not all! A wife is to remain the glamorous sex symbol, the understanding companion, the patient, untiring queen of the castle. There will be moments when the king will become a bit tarnished and you would like to have him abdicate — at least for the moment.

Remember when you were first engaged? You were absolutely sure that you had found a very special man. He would be strong but gentle, firm enough to protect you but never stubborn enough to prevent you from doing anything you really wanted to do. There would be flowers, gifts, candlelight and romance, compliments and appreciation. Sure, there would be problems, but you would talk them over and solve them together.

All too soon you discovered that you can't live on love. The bills have a way of coming due. Two cannot live as cheaply as one, and then there are three!

Prices begin escalating; long hours, weariness, and disappointments have a way of taking their toll.

One of the first acute disillusionments in marriage is the lack of freedom. Before marriage you looked forward to being free of parental demands. Indeed, you anticipated making your own rules and living as you pleased. Then you discovered that your husband had the same idea! He would make his own rules and determine what should be done. You found you had just switched dad for lad and opened under new management!

There always has been and always will be some type of authority over our lives. In formal education, there are teachers. In the outside world, there are police and legal restrictions. There are doctors governing the physical and pastors guiding the spiritual, and we chafe against the restricting influence. Yet we accept most of them as necessary, and at times are even grateful for many of them, especially when we gain from the protective benefits of their authority.

But there is one authority over our life that we seldom consider and of whom we often are not even aware. It is the controlling, loving guidance and provision of God. Often we think "If I didn't have to live with such a rebellious child, or a critical husband, or that nosy neighbor, or that outlawed in-law. . . . If they were different, I would never be critical of them." Did you know that the hardest person you must live with, the one who seems most critical, harsh, unfair, and demanding of you, may be God's choice gift to you?

Security in Forgiveness

It is only through exposure to situations that tax our very being that we truly learn forgiveness. If we have nothing to forgive, how can we ever experience the joy of rising above the level of resentfulness? How we long to stand on top of the mountain and look down, but we would prefer that there were no valleys or climbing involved! Yet the muscles of faith are developed in climbing, in reaching. God does not want His children to be spiritually anemic. If we live on nothing but rich foods, we become physically ill, and there is a spiritual parallel.

We are concerned with comfort and outward appearances while God is developing the inward beauty. It is done through the appointment of authority to whom we are to be in respectful obedience. If we resist the authority that God has placed over our lives, our children will resist the authority of our leadership and guidance of their lives.

Repeatedly, God has given this absolute: "Whatever a man sows, that he will also reap" (Galatians 6:7). That which we do to others, in one way or another, will be done to us. We have God's unconditional guarantee on this.

God has given clear-cut commands for the resolving of personal conflicts that will work without fail.

He does not intend us to be fearful, bitter, disillusioned, or unfulfilled in any way.

There are *no* perfect marriages, for there are no perfect people. No person has ever had all of the love and tenderness that she would like to have or feels that she needs. No one! No one person ever totally meets the needs of another. We are so constantly changing in our responses and reactions that if anyone should discover how to meet all our needs today, they would be different tomorrow. But we can learn some basic truths that will enable us to find a happy, satisfying, communicative relationship.

Security in Completeness

Deep in the heart of every person is a longing to become a complete person. There is an awareness of certain lacks and a longing to find someone who can fill them. Often we are drawn to people who are opposite us in personality, attitudes, and actions. The gay, bubbly, lighthearted girl who finds conversation so easy enjoys dating a fellow who listens in quiet admiration to her chatter. The thrifty, conservative girl enjoys the easy-come-easy-go fellow who takes her out to those frighteningly expensive places that she may brag about to others. After all, it's a nice arrangement. She can enjoy saving her money and spending his! The sensitive, creative girl who works beautifully with art, music, and colors may respond to the outgoing, confident leader. Sometimes the reverse is true. It is the man who has the artistic quality who chooses the organizationally oriented girl. They find their inner longings complemented by their differences.

Until marriage! In the close daily process of living together those differences become irritants, for they demand the giving of personality. We must adapt to each other and to change is to become insecure. We are frightened and hurt that anyone should think we *need* to change. Hurt produces anger.

It is at this point that we feel perhaps we need to "help" our husbands — for their own good, of course. They must learn to see things from the right point of view — our view. But, in the meantime, they are doing the same thing. Admiration begins to dwindle while criticism increases. The problem is, we begin to look quite human to one another. We begin to wonder if there could possibly be some mistake. How could such a sharp, intelligent, beautiful, talented girl become tied to a fellow who is obviously impatient, inconsiderate, stubborn, and selfish? He certainly had a girl fooled!

Communication dies under criticism, and the love light fades as the fuel of self-pity feeds the torch of anxiety and discontent. Anxiety flares when we conclude that a need is not being met or that a problem is not being solved. We look at the problem instead of at the God of the problem, and we seek our own solution. We know certain facts intellectually, but to translate those concepts into daily experience is vastly different.

In theory, we trust God; we want to lean hard on

Him. But deep inside is this insidiously disguised button that lights up whenever things do not go our way. We find ourselves manipulating people and things in order that life may be easier for self. But God loves us far too much to let us get away with it, for He knows it won't work! If we could change others as we want, it would be our own self-destruct button. It would annihilate the very desires of others to give to us that which we need most for balance and completeness. We cannot mold husbands and children into the "image of God," for we do not know what image He has in mind for them! It would only be a shabby image of our own design.

There is a vacuum in each life that will never be filled until it is filled by God Himself. It is the unrecognized longing for Him that motivates us to reach out to be a total person. We cannot fill satisfactorily the place that is reserved for Him with anyone or anything. Only when He has the unconditional freedom to occupy and direct our lives will we have perfect peace. If we are still making the final decisions, then God is not yet occupying that place.

God *is* God. He has perfect love and knowledge of each need. He will control people, places, and circumstances, especially husbands, when we remove the resistance of self-management. Then we are free to enjoy His efforts!

When God lays out a specific guideline and commands us to adjust our lives to its specifications, He takes the full responsibility for the results of that action, and it will *always* be for our best interest and ultimate happiness. It is the provision for our emancipation, that we may enjoy being God's women!

Togetherness has become a popular word in recent years, but the concept of oneness was given long ago when Adam received his bride from the hand of the Father (Genesis 2:24). The sex relationship should be reserved for this complete union of two people who, in the giving of themselves to one another, become "one flesh." It is the blending together of emotions, wills, spirit, and personality and all that we are. It is in becoming one with each other and with God that we find supreme happiness as we bring completeness to each other.

The first woman was created from Adam's rib. No doubt it is a reminder that she had her beginning nearest his heart, under his arm of protection. She was not intended to become the authority over him, nor was she to be trodden under foot by him. Hers was the precious place of being by his side, neither running ahead nor lagging behind, neither pushing nor pulling, but supporting.

We refer to the Church — that is, all persons who know the reality of sins forgiven, of having received Jesus Christ as Savior — as the bride of Christ. This bride was brought into being through the wounded side of Jesus Christ on Calvary as He gave His life for her. The needs of the Church, His bride, are identical with those of women today. His bride needs conversation with the bridegroom, Jesus Christ. We speak of this activity as prayer. She needs to walk under His arm of protection, hearing His heartbeat of love daily through the study of His Word. If it can be said that Jesus Christ as the Bridegroom has a need, it would be the recognition of His headship in our lives. Our worship of Him is predicated upon this fact.

This headship is often evidenced in the lives of women who have relinquished the privilege of marriage and motherhood that they might offer an undivided availability to God for His specific service. Henrietta Mears and others have left a dynamic impact on the lives of millions as they have experienced the direct fulfilling activity of Jesus Christ apart from the administrative role of a husband.

Some of the most beautiful lives of vibrant faith are those of women who have discovered in widowhood that the promises of God are not mere concepts. In Isaiah 54:4, 5, God uses this relationship to teach the nation Israel precious truths. "Fear not, for you will not be ashamed; be not confounded, for you will not be put to shame; for you will forget the shame of your youth, and the reproach of your widowhood you will remember no more. For your Maker is your husband, the Lord of hosts is his name; and the Holy One of Israel is your Redeemer, the God of the whole earth he is called."

God, through the Holy Spirit, assumes the responsibilities of a husband to those who need wisdom for business decisions, fellowship in loneliness, comfort and security in proving the reality that "your Maker is your husband."

Many women have rich spiritual insight that has been developed through consistent prayer communication and Bible study. They have a tender, responsive longing for the direction of God in their lives. For those of us who are wives, God has appointed a channel through whom He will reveal His purposes and initiate administrative decisions. He has not chosen this channel because of its perfection or merit in any sense. A woman has need of a visible head, and God has made provision for that need. As she accepts and uses that provision, God takes the responsibility for her and the results of her act of faith. Let us take a look at the first wife and see how that need was first made known.

In Eden, God spoke directly to Adam who was created before the woman. He instructed him in his responsibilities as caretaker of the earth and its environment. He also gave him spiritual instructions. All the fruit of the trees of the fabulous garden planted by God for their enjoyment was given to them, with the exception of one clearly defined tree. That tree was unique, for the fruit contained the knowledge of good and evil.

All that God had given to mankind was good, but the knowledge of evil was forbidden. It would mar his life with sin, disease, and, ultimately, death. This knowledge had been sealed in the container of fruit and pointed out as the one thing to be left to the wisdom of God. Adam had shared this instruction with Eve, as evidenced by her knowledge when temptation came.

Eve was easy prey to the suggestion prompted by Satan, and she determined to take what God, in His love, had forbidden. As her husband approached her, she encouraged him to join her in deliberate disobedience.

In guilt and fear they found themselves cowering in the bushes when God came to them. We are often led to believe that He walked daily with them in the garden, but the Bible does not say that. *After* they had sinned and were in hiding, He came to them in their need, sought them, and called them out. He opened the door of confession, and He is still doing the same today. The punishment for sin is death. God, in giving His Son, Jesus Christ, fulfilled the death penalty on Calvary. He calls to us in our deepest needs that He might reveal Himself in His forgiveness, love, and provision.

For Adam and Eve that provision was based on new conditions for their life together. The serpent had received the curse of being the instrument of Satan in deceiving the woman. The earth would bear the curse of man's sin with a crop that it had never produced before — weeds and thorns. Adam would find that providing for his family would be hard, physical work, "By the sweat of the brow" (Genesis 3:19). It has been the inborn sense of responsibility of man to do so ever since. It is the fear of failure to achieve this purpose that has become his barometer of success, often in a runaway excess of a God-given instinct. It is He who gives us the desire to do that which He commands us to perform. Experience and environment may distort those desires, but the basic urge is given by God.

God also spoke to Eve, "In pain you shall bring forth children; yet your desire shall be for your husband, and he shall rule over you" (Genesis 3:16, *New American Standard Bible*). Pain was a new experience, and in childbirth it would be a continual reminder of the efforts of Satan to disrupt and destroy the relationship of people to the God who loved them — a relationship that would one day be restored through a Child born of woman. Yet in spite of personal pain, Eve would desire her husband's affection and recognize his leadership.

There is a rich parallel between the spiritual family of God and successful, happy, family relationships. In Ephesians we read, "You wives *must* submit to your husbands' leadership *in the same way* you submit to the Lord. For a husband is in charge of his wife in the same way Christ is in charge of his body the church. . . . *you wives must willingly obey your husbands in everything, just as the church obeys Christ.* And you husbands, show the same kind of love to your wives as Christ showed to the church when he died for her. . . . the wife must see to it that she deeply respects her husband — obeying, praising and honoring him" (Ephesians 5:22–25, 33, *Living Bible*).

I have discovered, as a wife, that God's commands to me are *not* conditional. My obedience is not contingent upon the personality or performance of my husband. The requirement is simply to believe God enough to do what He has said and trust the end results to Him. God cannot bless deliberate disobedience. I do not have a *natural* desire to have anyone, even a good husband, rule over me, nor do I want to "submit" to the headship of another. But God has developed a marvelous harmony and love for one another in our home as we have discovered that this command frees us from self and many aspects of selfishness. Competition for supremacy may be an important stimulus in many organizations, but in the home it can produce deadly conflicts, tensions, and frustrations. Creative ideas, desires, and dreams should be shared with each other, but God has appointed one top administrator who is responsible to Him for final decisions and provisions.

Security in Self-Knowledge

Many voices question the role of women today, and perhaps you, too, are searching for your identity. What are you really like as God's custom-designed creation? You are totally unique, for there is no one like you in the whole wide world! You are to have the priceless privilege of molding the life of that dear baby whom your arms may hold one day. If God does not give you that privilege, it is because He has chosen a better thing for you. But He will equip you with exactly the right abilities that you need for every responsibility and opportunity that He gives.

You are given the rich expressive treasure of emotions, but they will need to be guarded, not allowed to rule over you. You delight in the flame of sunset across a twilight sky, the harmony of music, poetry, and art, and all that is creative. You are graceful and intuitive, with longings and deep needs. The man has never lived who can fully understand and meet the quickly changing needs of your life. And if he could, you would be bored to tears.

Your world is a world of people. A child cries in the night and you rise to respond. You have the ability to recognize and react to people and their needs. Your thoughts are definite, fine details with practical solutions to issues, but they may be colored by feelings rather than fact, for you often think in terms of emotions and feelings.

God gives to each the ability to perform that which He has ordained. As we discover His basic purpose and design for us, we will find the ability to achieve it. A woman is usually happiest when her world revolves around meeting the needs of real people here and now, while a man often prefers the statistical approach to world-wide issues. Perhaps you have seen this occur in everyday happenings.

Have you ever gone house hunting with a man? It can be a shattering, frustrating experience. While looking for a place to live one day, our searching led us to a lovely old home that I just adored. There was a quaint little dining room with windows opening out toward the sunset. The upstairs bedrooms with their little slanted roofs would be just perfect to use for the boys. I could visualize our furniture with the soft burnt-orange carpets. But I was crushed with disappointment when Hal crawled out from under the house and said simply, "Dry rot. We would have to put in new flooring in a couple of years, probably even new wiring. And did you see those tiny bedrooms upstairs? A fellow can't even stand up straight in them. Can't you imagine our boys when they are teen-agers walking with a bend in their back to clear the ceiling?"

The battle was on as I painted a mental picture of the charm and comfort of the house here and now, but the matter was resolved when he calmly said, "Honey, I have to earn the money to pay the bills when we change these things. It is not the house for us." Sadly enough, he was right. Later we found a much nicer house and were in complete agreement about it. God had used Hal's "facts and figures" thinking to protect us from a bad investment, while it was the creativity God has given me that enabled us to recognize and develop the fullest potential of the house that eventually became our home. In our combined abilities the best interest of our family was met.

Not only do we think differently as women, but our needs are different. Conversation and the opportunity to express emotions and have them accepted, along with being loved and appreciated, top the list. You need freedom in many ways, and yet security and the knowledge that you are needed are important too. You especially enjoy being *told* that you are loved.

Your husband needs to have the admiration, respect, and gratitude that belong to one who is the supply and directive power behind the home. I certainly have felt a twinge of envy when the "girl next door" oozes her appreciation and admiration all over my husband while he fixes her flat tire and mine still waits! She looks up and sweetly murmurs, "Oh, I wish my husband would do things like you do!" Secretly, I may need to put aside visions of arsenic as I think, "I wish *my* husband would too!"

But what happened the last time he tried? Was my response, "Well, it's about time!" Was I perhaps a little critical of the way in which it was done?

A man *must* have admiration from someone, for it is a God-given need. Since you share your emotions, why not share your appreciation and admiration? It is easy to forget that a husband has worked long hours away from home, often in highly competitive circumstances that threaten even a continuation of that job. Gratitude for those efforts is important. Even the worst of us have something that can be admired sincerely! Nothing kills communication, cooperation, and consideration as quickly as criticism and a judgmental attitude.

Perhaps one of our biggest problems is the misuse of conversation. It is amazing how we lock deep within ourselves the really important things that we feel and are — especially the tender, kind impulses that we stifle. It is a badly directed effort to protect ourselves from possible rejection or hurt. We develop our own unique code system and feel terribly hurt when it is not properly translated to produce the desired results.

I first discovered this one night when a large number of guests had left our home and I began clearing away things in the kitchen. Suddenly I felt my husband's arm around my shoulders as he said, "Honey, what's wrong?"

Surprised, I said, "Nothing is wrong. Absolutely nothing!"

He laughed and said, "I have learned that when you begin banging pans and dishes, you are upset. Now what is it all about?"

I had not realized it, but I *was* annoyed by the remarks of a guest that evening. My husband knew me better than I knew myself! He had deciphered the code that I didn't even know existed!

There are many occasions when we send out our messages, totally unaware that we are doing so. A birthday is forgotten, and the coded message to husband may say, "There's a hamburger in the oven for your dinner. I have a headache and have gone to bed early." Decoded it would read, "You rascal! You don't deserve even a cold hamburger. I would rather cover up my head than have to see anyone who is so selfish and thoughtless that he wouldn't take me to dinner on my birthday!"

Typically enough, we are usually the last to know that we have so disguised our real message. We seldom know why we feel so bad or so frustrated. When we sort out the reason and can express it in a loving way that does not make another person feel guilty, both will be happy. The air is cleared. For instance, better results would have been achieved by saying, "You may be the busiest man in town, but birthdays only come once a year. Wouldn't you like to take me out to dinner?" The truth is, most men do not break the code or get the message we are sending, for they think in terms of facts. So give them the facts on which you want them to act.

Too often, conversation is used to belittle another. Man's greatest fear is fear of failure. He fears failing to provide adequately for his family, failing to be the husband and father whom he can respect. There are men who have suffered such severe psychological wounds early in childhood that they may show an unwillingness to take on the financial responsibility or headship of the home. They have been so conditioned as a child that they are not capable of succeeding. Continued criticism or belittling on the part of a wife would only insure refusal to try. Encouragement, gentle confidence, and love can be blended for healing of those wounds.

We should never make comparisons that deride a husband's capabilities. Nature builds in the instinct to hide from possible confrontation with failure. For a man, those attempts at escape may take various forms. It may be a retreat of stony silence, especially if his opinions or suggestions have been refused or criticized. It may simply be to sit in a restaurant and chat with other customers and waitresses who will hear him. He may choose a joint escape with other men who have similar problems and have learned to fill their vacuum with poker parties, sex films, or illicit relationships. Alcohol and drugs are common escapes. Sometimes an intensive throwing of oneself into work, social, or religious activity in an abnormal excess are ways out. Dangerous sports to an extreme or even criminal activity (theft, not based on financial need, but a means of proving cleverness) are other ways. The extreme outlets may be shown in brutality to women in an effort to refute their feelings of failure, or in mental withdrawal from reality. Thoughts of and attempts at suicide may be the end result.

How wonderfully abundant is the provision for every failure, real or imagined, in each life as Jesus Christ invites us to place it in His dear hands, to relinquish it and receive forgiveness and peace. The failures of the past cannot be changed. They can be forgiven, but the future will depend upon what we do with them today.

There are tremendous rewards of happiness waiting for us when we discipline our memory in "Forgetting what lies behind and straining forward to what lies ahead" (Philippians 3:13). The end result of living in the past is often the destruction of the future, a future that all too often ends in separation or divorce.

The major cause of divorce in America today is seldom stated. We have developed many euphemisms for it, while we ignore the real problem.

Stated simply, incompatability means that the needs of husband and wife are not being met by one another. In most cases, needs have not been met because one or both partners have not understood those needs from the other partner's point of view. Each then waits for the other to change his or her behavior pattern (with a few not-so-helpful pushes) and to meet those needs, but somone must initiate all action.

People will initiate divorce proceedings before they will initiate the building of satisfying marriage relationships. Divorce imposes blame on one or both partners and can be legislated. Building requires a giving of self and can only be achieved through living experience.

Marriage does not create problems, but it does turn the spotlight of stress and pressure upon the flaws and unresolved conflicts within our personalities and brings them to the surface where they are exposed and amplified. Marriage collapses when each person focuses his or her attention upon the rights to have needs met and judges and condemns the seeming failure of the mate to do so. How we resent being robbed! So does our marriage partner! Just plain common courtesy and healthy personal grooming with the right appreciation of timing can solve many problems.

The most important minutes of a day are the first five in the morning when we awaken and become aware of each other. Those impressions are indelibly burned in our mind: the way we look, the tone of voice, and, most of all, the attitude. Next in importance are the first five minutes when we meet each other after having been separated by the hours of the working day.

The nicest thing you can do to show love at that moment is to have an atmosphere of "Welcome" ready and waiting, to be neat and attractive, and to smell fresh and wholesome. Have the aroma of fresh-perked coffee and dinner in preparation, and have the children clean and busy at play without a sense of frantic hurry and disorder.

A man in counseling said one evening, "I think the sweetest thing in this world must be to put your hand on the doorknob and know that just on the other side is someone waiting who loves you. That makes all the guff at the office worthwhile. Who wants a scribbled note and a TV dinner? Why put in fifty hours of pressure a week for that? What do I want most in this world? I want a wife who is happy! If she's happy, I know I'm doing all right. But I just want her around — not always off at some club meeting.

"Why should a man have to take a broom and sweep a path between the laundry baskets and the toys? My wife used to work in an office; she was an efficient organizer, and she always looked great. But when she quit work and started staying home, she never cleaned up — not for me at any rate. Maybe if she has a club to go to, but not for me. Even the kids are always yelling and dirty. Why should a guy have to change diapers the first five minutes he's in the house? I don't think it's a question of time. I think it's a matter of caring."

The motivation of caring is a strong one. It is caring enough to set priorities on our time. It is the caring of God for you and your family that has prompted such infinite care in designing a plan that will give you the happiness for which you long. He will lift the burden of unnecessary responsibility that bends your back and exhausts your mind and spirit. There is deep and marvelous security in discovering that God does not depend upon or permit us to change one another as we might desire. For then it would surely destroy the balance that we need. In combining the thrifty and the generous, stinginess and selfishness are prevented. The cautious and the daring blend to bring balance. It takes the doer and the dreamer to have the vision and the follow-through to achieve.

The joy lies in welcoming the differences and drawing upon them as resources and reservoirs of new vitality and interest. It is the Potter who has molded both, and His design is perfect. He takes the responsibility for the wife who trusts His plan of headship. God is the ultimate Head of the family on earth even as He is in heaven, molding the earthly family to the image of the heavenly one through His appointed head, the husband. It is the beginning of real security to rest in Him for all of our needs, for none are contingent upon the goodness or the performance of anyone but God Himself. We do not deserve heaven, but He has made it available to us as His love-gift. We have the privilege of freeing others to realize their fullest potential as we allow them to be led directly by God, even though it is a sacrifice of love to remove our hands.

Security in Submission

Like Sarah, the wife of Abraham, we learn that our trust is in God, but our submission is to the husband whom God has appointed the family head under His direction. The prefix "sub" usually indicates a person who is in secondary position of authority or service. A mission is a designated work or errand of representation. Submission surely is the designated work of representing God through willingness to be second in authority in the home that is under God. Then He alone carries the responsibility for our well-being.

"*In the same spirit* (See 1 Peter 2:21-25) you married women should adapt yourselves to your husbands, so that even if they do not obey the Word of God they may be won to God without any word being spoken, simply by seeing the pure and reverent behaviour of you, their wives. Your beauty should not be dependent on an elaborate coiffure, or on the wearing of jewelry or fine clothes, but on the inner personality — the unfading loveliness of a calm and gentle spirit, a thing very precious in the eyes of God. This was the secret of the beauty of the holy women of ancient times who trusted in God and were submissive to their husbands" (1 Peter 3:1-5, *Phillips*).

There is no freedom or security for the person who feels that he must protect his own rights and see to it that his own needs are met. Not one of us can ever adequately protect himself from hurts, disappointments, and seeming losses. As long as we struggle to do so, self is the central focus of attention — a self that is becoming increasingly apprehensive, resentful, and filled with self-pity and insecurity. The inverted focus is looking inward to the limitations that have produced the failures of the past.

It is only when we turn our confidence and the focus of our thoughts and hopes upon Jesus Christ and His unlimited love and protection that we find a marvelous security that cannot be shaken. *He loves us. He will take care of every area of our life that we relinquish into His hands. He will not fail us.*

The key to security lies in confidence in God's character of love. The things that are happening to us are not accidents. They are designed by the hand of God that we may develop new and beautiful character traits, new depths of understanding, of forgiveness, of love for others, of compassion — that we may explore the riches of our heavenly Father's family treasury.

One day I stood outside an office door. The door was locked, and no one was there. Inside that room were all of the materials I needed to accomplish an important task. Looking at the keys in my hand, I felt a deep sense of frustration. A new door had just been installed, and I had the keys to the old door. What good were they in this situation?

Then a voice spoke to me. "June, you have the key to the door. It is the same door that was on the old library. Try using it." Turning, I saw the smiling face of an old friend. Thrusting the key into the lock, I found the door swung open wide. There were all the supplies that I needed, just waiting to be used.

The same faith that brought you to trust Jesus Christ for salvation is the key to this new door. If you have had confidence in His love and forgiveness of sin, can you not have confidence in His power to control the people, places, and circumstances that you face at this moment? Even a seemingly impossible marriage?

God sent a messenger to a young woman long ago to tell her that "with God nothing will be impossible" (Luke 1:37). This is the message I bring you today. There is happiness and security, beyond any of your wildest dreams, available to you as you plunge deep into the richness of God's love that transforms our "impossible situations" into the delight of His presence. As your life becomes truly "open under new management," the management of God takes the responsibility for your future.

> *"With God nothing will be impossible"*
> (Luke 1:37).

"Peace I leave with you. . . . Let not your hearts be troubled, neither let them be afraid" (John 14:27).

4
Step Back and Discover Peace

God has a fantastic gift for you! A gift that will flood your thoughts with brightness and your daily routine with delight. Your future is as bright as the promises of God when you discover His gift of peace. Peace is a bridge between the past and the future — a future yet unknown. Peace is more than an absence of friction. It is a positive calm that is not lost in the turbulence of change or trouble. It is an inward harmony that produces strength for today.

It has been said that most of us are crucified daily between two thieves. One is guilt and regret for yesterday and the other is fear and anxiety for tomorrow. Both rob us of the treasure of this moment. Only today *is*! Looking back causes marriage and other important life relationships to become sour and dull, if not an open warfare. Plush carpets, fast cars, beautiful homes, and impressive bank accounts do not produce peace or happiness, nor does their absence bring inward harmony.

Have you ever had the feeling, as I have, that there must be some strange subtle conspiracy to prevent you from really doing what you want to do or having what you want? For example, there's the girl in the television series: Her clothes are beautiful. Her hair is styled just the right way to take advantage of every good feature. Her home is an interior decorator's dream. Her children are well-mannered. And just look at her husband! He takes her out to dinner while you dream up fifty ways to fix hamburger! It doesn't seem fair at times. We know that the situation isn't real, but it is certainly ideal! Why shouldn't we have a tiny bit of life like that? We look at our feelings and sometimes overlook the facts as they really are. There is a way to find harmony between the actual facts of our life and the way that we see it through the cloud of our emotions or feelings.

The Peace of Honesty and Forgiveness

Many of our feelings of being unappreciated, unloved, or unfairly treated stem from a delinquent bookkeeping system. It is easy to look backward at the events and of people who have been involved in my life in the past. If I think of them in terms of old hurts, failures, and fears, they will be superimposed on todays' happenings: I will relive and recreate that past experience until my future becomes a repeat performance of that which God has already declared concealed and non-existent.

It is impossible to live with guilt and frustration over the past and experience peace for the present or hope for the future. Prominent men in medical fields believe that much physical illness is psychosomatic and that the hormone system has the ability to serve as a protective defense system for the body. When the emotions and attitudes are out of adjustment, the defensive action is hindered. Effort is then made to cope with that particular problem. It is possible for the emotional system to blot out certain events that become too painful to remember. Temporary blindness, deafness, or a variety of other conditions can result.

But buried things do have a way of coming to the surface sooner or later. And it is these buried guilts that smolder and grow which produce the most disastrous physical, emotional, and spiritual diseases.

That's the way it was with Jennifer. She was attractive, talented, a marvelous organizer and administrator. Her faith seemed to scale mountains, as did her kindness. The greater the difficulty, the greater seemed her endurance. There were many problems in her home, and at times she worked full-time jobs to compensate for the lack of other income. Conflicts with growing teen-agers and a daughter in prison were added heartbreaks.

Eventually her life began changing. Her husband found a good job and soon they had an excellent income. They bought a lovely home and all the things money could provide. The daughter in prison came to know the reality of Christ as Savior, and she began working with other women in prison. When she was released, she continued to show the compassion and understanding to those who had such needs.

One day Jennifer's husband called me and said, "Something is happening to my wife, and I am concerned. She is so depressed. Unless something is done, I'm afraid she may have to be placed in a mental hospital."

Shortly after that Jennifer and I had lunch together. It was hard to believe that the warm, cheerful friend I had known for so many years had become the despondent, disinterested woman who hardly glanced at me. We talked about many things, even early childhood days in a small eastern town. We saw each other often after that, and then one day I asked her what was the most frightening thing that ever happened to her as a child.

She talked about a mother and dad who were cold and aloof to one another. She spoke of things that had been forgotten for years, and then she said, "There was one terrible day when dad locked the cellar door." She poured out a story of hatred for her father. He had had sexual experimentation with her when she was tiny and had then bribed her with gifts not to tell her mother.

She said, "No one ever found out about it. I was never punished. But I have always hated my body. I've gone from one extreme to another: sometimes totally neglecting my appearance; at other times choosing clothes that would be ultrasmart as a compensation. I had to do things better than anyone else in order to have people like me. The discipline of our children has been unstable. I have let them get away with everything until it accumulated to such a pressure point that I would lose all self-control and punish them for no apparent reason. I have learned the difference between punishment and discipline but only after a great deal of damage was done. Their lives have been a playback of my problems. Perhaps it has been an unconscious effort on their part to punish themselves for those things I have ignored."

Conscience is a wonderful thing. It is an early warning system that demands instant correction of the malfunction of thoughts and actions to protect us from damage of accumulated failures or conflicts. It demands one of two alternatives: forgiveness or punishment. If we do not satisfy the instinct for punishment through people, places, and happenings, we will inflict our own and experience the loss of self-respect.

Jennifer realized that when things were difficult she could rise to the challenge, for it was in the very suffering of those situations that her buried sense of guilt was relieved. She did not have the capacity for happiness while carrying the burden of early childhood problems. She felt that she did not deserve and could not tolerate prosperity. She had endured the destructive activity of inverted pride: the longing for personal perfection. Failing to find it, she rejected the person that she saw herself to be.

Healing begins when we see ourselves as we are: a person who is not and never will be perfect on this earth, but one who is loved and valued by God and is of value to others. There is no way that we can punish self and become rid of guilt. We must see guilt for what it is and recognize that Jesus Christ has taken the punishment for it in order that He might give us full forgiveness, restoration, and recovery.

Jennifer discovered the joy of release, the freedom of honesty and forgiveness and its resulting peace. Her father was no longer a man to be hated but an old man with emotional and spiritual illness. Having received forgiveness from God, she could now forgive those whom she had resented. The walls that had been built by deception would be torn down, and love and communication could flow openly. The capacity to enjoy the good things provided by a loving husband and a tremendous God were just beginning!

The Danger of Unresolved Guilt

Not all of the attempts at self-punishment result from forgotten issues, but often we do not recognize the reason or the ineffectiveness of our actions. A man who built a lifetime of such an existence was a well-known beggar in Lahore, India. When he was just a boy, he began forging a chain about his body. He believed that by doing so he was being punished for every wrong action and attitude of his life. Day by day he added new links. As the years went by, it became so heavy that he could only crawl through the filth of the streets, dragging his self-imposed robe of chains. The last few years of his life he carried the weight of over 650 pounds of chains. He died never having known freedom from them. A life that could have been filled with peace and positive achievement ended in useless bondage.

Each person handles guilt in one of three ways:

1) By repressing or burying guilt knowingly or unconsciously.
2) By expressing guilt in the right or wrong way.
3) By confessing guilt and discovering forgiveness and freedom.

Both the beggar and Jennifer suffered intensely from unresolved guilt. Through the years, Jennifer had confessed surface guilts (the little daily failures) many times and found surface relief, but the deeper guilt was still buried in her memory. For a period of time she had forgotten that it had ever happened, but she still suffered the results of it! It is the hidden, forgotten-for-the-moment conflicts of the past that often cause that vague sense of apprehension, of coming disaster. These worries and fears rob us of the bouyant hope, the excited expectation of having God do something marvelous in our lives. They are feelings that prevent us from valuing ourselves as persons.

Kathy shared this same type of experience with me one evening as she said, "I have met a tremendous Christian fellow, and we are planning to be married. But I am so frightened at times. What if our love doesn't last? What if I am not a good wife? He may not love me after we have been married for a while." The teacup in her hands began trembling as she spoke of her fears for their future. But as she talked, she began to realize that underneath the fears was the memory of an earlier romance that had ended in pregnancy. Like a towering giant, her guilt loomed between her and future happiness.

She had found temporary relief in putting the blame upon the boy. "If he had not been so attentive, so persuasive, it never would have happened."

Isn't it a terrific temptation to "pass the buck" and justify our actions and attitudes by placing the blame on others?

Last week two special little grandsons came to spend the day with me. Just as they arrived, I pulled a pan of hot cookies from the oven. Then I left the room to answer the phone. When I came back, Danny said, "Grandma June, Eric took some of your cookies." Danny was very quiet as we sat and munched cookies and milk together. Then smiling up at me shyly, he said, "Grandma, I took your cookies too."

I put my arms around him and hugged him and said, "Danny, I baked them for you. I am so glad that you told me what you did. Now we can both enjoy them together." Suddenly it was as if sunshine filled the room. That warm, sweet freedom of loving and being loved, of being secure enough to say, "I was wrong."

We smile at the ruse of a child to escape the responsibility for his actions, but often our reactions are just a more sophisticated attempt to do the same thing. How our dear Savior wants us to know we are safe with Him and can trust His love and forgiveness. We do not need to expose the faults and guilts of others.

Matthew 7:1-5 tells us: "Don't criticize people, and you will not be criticized. For you will be judged by the way you criticize others, and the measure you give will be the measure you receive.

"Why do you look at the speck of sawdust in your brother's eye and fail to notice the plank in your own? How can you say to your brother, 'Let me get the speck out of your eye,' when there is a plank in your own? You fraud! Take the plank out of your own eye first, and then you can see clearly enough to remove your brother's speck of dust." *(Phillips)*.

Repression.
Expression.
Confession.

How can I express those things that hurt me — those things that make me feel as if I have failed? Why do so many plans seem to fail?

Recently, Hal and I celebrated our thirty-first wedding anniversary. We drove through a heavy rainstorm to the lodge at the top of the mountain. It had been a temptation to cancel our dinner reservation because of the storm, but as we were seated by the window overlooking the spectacular Snoqualmie Falls, the clouds parted. Blue skies began appearing. In a few minutes there was a breathtaking sunset, and a rainbow added its assurance that the rains were over.

The chill gray of wind and rain had threatened disappointment for the moment, but the flaming glory of the clouds outlined in red and gold far surpassed a calm unclouded sky. Our life together through the years has been that way too. We thought of all the dreams and plans we had had at the beginning of our married life. Almost none of them had ever been fulfilled. There had been hundreds of temporary disappointments because our hopes were focused upon *our* plans — *our* dreams. But in every instance we discovered that our Lord had replaced each with a far better, more exciting and rewarding adventure. Every plan which God tossed aside as inadequate was replaced with a far better one.

The years have been stormy, but we have discovered the only security we have or ever shall have is in God's planning for us. His plans include His provision for every need of our lives. Our plans will fail, but His never fail! We may go down into the valley again, and there will be more storms, but eventually we will see that final sunrise when we are with the Son Himself.

So many families have come to us with intense marriage conflicts as a result of having had beautiful dreams that were never fulfilled. Finding their goals fading away unachieved, they blamed their marriage partner for the seeming failures.

Fear of failure as a parent or a mate can cause a person to become suspicious and lose communication with others. It is such a temptation to justify these feelings by enlisting support through the opinion of others. As the inward conflict is passed on to those who are not involved, it is as if social and emotional disease cells are being circulated. Additional lives are drawn into an ever-widening circle of disease, and they must take sides either for or against those involved.

How it rocks the world of a child when his parents try to prove each other wrong in the happenings of family life, whether it is the use of funds, child discipline, promptness for meals, use of leisure time, or a thousand other issues. A child's security is terribly threatened if he must choose sides. When he agrees with mom, he is guilty of deserting dad, and vice versa. Inwardly, that child becomes a divided person, for there is no way he can remain untouched. The emotional thermostat of a home can get pretty hot when each person throws valuable energy into protecting his pet peeve, especially a peeve based on past failure which generates fear that it may occur again.

Wouldn't it be great if we could say what we feel without causing a real blow-up? We can and should clear the air of minor static before it becomes a major explosion. Can you imagine what would happen if each person could learn to share objectively those things that he feels without causing others to feel guilty or accused? When we are accused or feel we have failed, we must retaliate, and the fight is on! What a difference it can make when seeming failures are rightly understood as prized opportunities for learning and growth!

This is the way just such an incident happened in our home one crisp autumn morning. The sound of a car coming up the drive was suddenly interrupted by a resounding crash! Then there was Hal, looking a bit sheepish as he spoke teasingly, "You know that fence you've been wanting me to tear down? I just started! When I came down the drive, I must have hit some ice. The next thing I knew there was a great big hole in the fence. I'm glad of the warning that it's time to watch for ice. It could have been disasterous to have realized it on the freeway. And maybe this is just what I needed to make me take that fence down."

We had a good laugh together and were grateful

for the limited damage to the car. Hal did not suffer the agony of feeling that he was a careless driver. Instead he looked objectively at the facts, which were these:

1) The fence should be torn down.
2) He needed the motivation to get the project started.
3) It was a positive learning experience for his safety and protection.

He did not react against the facts with personal feelings but accepted them as a loving gift from God who cared about every detail of his day and life.

Here is a simple guideline to healthy, happy attitudes in facing the daily events of living.

1) Learn to view the facts objectively, *without condemning* or being critical of yourself or anyone else.
2) Recognize that it is a God-given opportunity for learning what will work toward your ultimate happiness and well-being.
3) Dress these experiences in the gay garb of humor and gratitude rather than the fearful expectation of some pending tragedy that probably never will occur.

In facing those things that would otherwise seem disappointments or failures, you open the door to communication, freedom, and peace. You discover that today is an independent segment of time. It does not lean back upon yesterday, nor does it bend forward to color tomorrow. You can stand tall in the glory and peace of the present.

The Peace of Confession and Healing

The positive, healthy experience of peace can become ours as we find freedom from guilt. Negatives of guilt will be transformed into positives when we simply confess, *without excuse*, our responsibility in conflicts.

Why is it so difficult to say, "I am wrong; I have failed"? That barrier of pride is a fantastically steep mountain to climb!

Several years ago, I discovered I had erected a "holy smoke screen" of self-protection to avoid the sharp reality of confessing guilt. After all, I reasoned, if I was in "Christian leadership," didn't I have a responsibility to those who looked to me for their example? I couldn't let them down! It might crush them to realize that I failed in many ways too.

Then I realized the truth: Jesus Christ is the only example anyone can ever have that will not eventually bring disillusionment. If I was not honest with my loved ones, my facade would hurt them much more than possible disappointment in my personality or performance. They were far more aware of my inconsistencies and imperfections than I could ever be — especially my husband and children and those exposed to me in pressure situations.

And what a marvelous secret I learned! As I no longer tried to protect my image before them, they were no longer critical of me. They were so kind, forgiving, and encouraging. Tears filled my eyes as I realized how beautiful and gracious their lives had become.

We can become honestly objective about ourselves and our motives and show confidence in the willingness of others to understand and forgive. There is an identification with others through mutual needs, not through idealistic perfection.

With whom do you have a greater bond? A friend with whom you have had a real chance to share and give of yourself, or with one who has no known needs? Friends who seem to value me most are those who have shared with me in one way or another. There is a richness of mutual sharing, of investing ourselves in one another. There is a giving of ourselves in trust to each other that builds genuine friendships and wholesome family relationships.

How wonderful the words of James 5:16: "Confess your sins to one another, and pray for one another, that *you* may be healed." Notice that it is the one who prays for others after having confessed his sins who receives healing.

Now, I want to take you with me on a special adventure in health and happiness. You will need a sheet of paper and a pencil.

First, determine the person with whom you have the most conflict. Perhaps it is someone who has hurt you deeply. Jot his/her name at the top of the page.

Remember all the standards, ideals, and longings you once had in mind for this person — especially in relationship to yourself. For instance, if you have written down your husband's name, you might feel he should be considerate, remembering birthdays and anniversaries. He should be protective when others abuse or criticize. Certainly his financial provision should be adequate. He should keep the touch of romance alive — say, "I love you." He should take responsibility in leadership and supervision with the children, but not in opposition to your ideas! He should assume spiritual leadership.

There are scores of other ideals for each person with whom we come in contact. An employer should be courteous and fair. We are disturbed by harsh, critical, impatient, or over-thrifty habits.

There are certain standards and characteristics that are acceptable to us in evaluating other parents, teachers, pastors, friends, relatives, children, and all life relationships. Needless to say, we are going to be disappointed in *every one of these areas if we have contact with any person long enough*. It is what we do with these disappointments that is tremendously important. And this brings us to the second step.

Write down all the things that you would like this person to have done, said, or been as your ideal husband, child, etc.

It will become quite apparent that the one with whom you share this relationship is far from what you envisioned.

Now, write down the shortcomings you see in his/her life. Tell it like it is, from *your* point of view. Just how has he/she disillusioned or disappointed you?

Wow! What a poor specimen. Have you missed anything? Remember, this is a spring cleaning of all the debris that has accumulated in the attic of your mind and heart. It is important that you clean the whole thing. Don't leave any skeletons rattling around!

Remember the three-point guide for healthy attitudes? Let's put it to work with this person and see the results.

1) *View the facts objectively without condemning self or others.*

Obviously other people are not all they could or should be, but why not enjoy the most worthwhile relationship possible with them? Do you believe that they think you are the kindest, most gracious person they would long for you to be? The simple fact is that both of you have dreams for one another which have not yet been fulfilled. You are changing and so are they. Each of you needs non-critical, understanding, compassionate acceptance of one another. Therefore, will you ask God to help you see and value this person from His point of view?

2) *Recognize this as a long-range opportunity that God may develop within your life beautiful character traits such as forgiveness, gentleness, patience, and encouragement.*

You are becoming a lovely person, a joy to all who know you and a delight to your Savior's heart. God is expanding His personality in your life. If you are limited in the ability to graciously forgive, He will arrange an opportunity or a need to demonstrate forgiveness. Someone will be unkind or hurtful to you so that you may experience the joy of becoming free of resentment. As you show genuine forgiveness, you will be healed and happy. No wonder God has said, "Happy are those who promote peace with one another."

It is important to recognize that most of our hurts are actually the reaction of our own feelings toward others. We *feel* unloved, unappreciated, and misunderstood, and we react against the person whom we feel is responsible.

Let's take a look at the list of faults you have noted. How do you feel about them?

Write down the hurts, resentments, disappointments, or other feelings you may have.

Feelings result from the combined attitudes and actions of our own personality. Probably you will discover that the exact opposite of the reaction you are feeling is the lovely character trait God wants to build in your life. This list can become your "tip sheet" to help you recognize and cooperate with His work in making your life beautiful. Wouldn't you like to get rid of any feelings which slow down that process? You can. After you have read this section, close your eyes and visualize the fact that Jesus Christ is right there with you.

Jesus is with you; He loves you and has a gift for you. In Isaiah 58:9 we read that, "If you take away from the midst of you (in the center of your life, within your personality, and in the center of your family and influence) the yoke, the pointing of the finger, and speaking wickedness," He will do marvelous things.

The "yoke" is the attempt to harness and cause heavy burdens. It is the opposite of being a free person, for it speaks of bondage.

The "pointing of the finger" speaks of criticism, of judging, of discouraging others. "Speaking wickedness" implies that when we point out to others how wrong they are or the inadequacies of their efforts, it is for the purpose of causing them to realize our superior capabilities.

In Isaiah 58:7 the tenderness of God's heart pleads with us, "Hide not yourself from your own flesh" (paraphrase). "Then shall your light break forth like the dawn and your healing shall spring up speedily. . . ." Do not hide yourself — your personality, your love, forgiveness, and gentleness, your faith and confidence. The thrilling promise of God that He will give "beauty for ashes" is found in Isaiah 61:3 *(King James Version)*. As you recognize the presence of Jesus with you, consider the reality of His hands held out to offer you beauty and happiness. They are empty hands. They are waiting to receive your deepest hurts. Will you give your list to Him? "As far as the east is from the west, so far does he remove our transgressions from us" (Psalm 103:12). It was the purpose of Christ's death on Calvary that you might have *all* sins forgiven and live a life at peace with God and man. It is His desire as the Prince of Peace to live in harmony within our lives, our homes.

It has been said that when sin is confessed and

relinquished into His dear hands, it is as if a sign was erected over even the remembrance of those things. On the sign are these words: "No Fishing Allowed." We are to build a memorial of praise over the spot where the old issues once existed. As a part of the groundwork for your new experience, take a match and light the paper you have written. Watch it burn until only the ashes remain. The paper is gone but, far more important, so is the guilt of wrong reactions. Even the ashes are to be given to Him that He may begin your first "beauty treatment." This is the beginning of "beauty for ashes"!

Isn't it wonderful to be fresh and free? If you are not, perhaps the person with whom you have the greatest difficulty is yourself! It may be a valuable opportunity to really get acquainted with you! Take a new sheet of paper and follow the very same steps, remembering to be completely honest about your own dreams for your life and the personal defeats you have experienced. Then go on to relax in God's arms. Anticipate, with confidence, discovering the reason He has permitted these experiences. Often it is so that we might learn to trust His ability and provision to handle every need. Sometimes it is that we might be of help to others who have deep needs, *especially the ones with whom we have had the deepest problems.*

Let's take a quick look at the third suggestion in building new attitudes and relationships.

3) *Recognize the importance of humor and gratitude in facing the future and opening communications with those with whom we have had conflicts.*

Isn't it amazing how difficult it is to take the initiative in restoring broken relationships? The longer we delay, the more difficult it becomes. We overemphasize the happenings that took place — especially the way we feel about others' opinions of us.

The flood of gratitude which fills our hearts when we have received Jesus Christ's forgiveness needs to be shared. It needs to be given to the person with whom we have had difficulty. There will be people whose forgiveness we need to ask.

Ask God to direct your thoughts in recognizing exactly who they are. Ask Him to prepare their attitudes for your visit or, if you cannot go, for your phone call. Choose only words that will express in the simplest way possible your desire for their forgiveness, especially words that will in *no way imply guilt on their part.*

So often we feel, "But they are wrong." Only the Spirit of God can reveal to them their need to discover His freedom. *Do not try to do God's work for Him.* Do the work He has commanded us to do: ask forgiveness. Explanations are only a way of excusing past failures; we no longer need excuses, for God has removed them! Explanations are a part of the dying struggle of pride to hold us and prevent us from knowing the peace and freedom this very action is designed to achieve. There is freedom from pride and self only when we are willing to let Jesus Christ put them under His feet. Then it will be His honesty and love that others will see in us. No longer can the desire to protect wounded pride enslave us.

The most difficult, and yet the most successful, request for forgiveness is the shortest. "I have been wrong. I am sorry. Will you forgive me?" Getting involved in specific details may only raise new issues and questions as well as tempt us to imply guilt to others. Be sure that you *ask* for their forgiveness and receive their reply. Their commitment of forgiveness is an investment in your life. They have spoken it, and their ears have recorded it. In the future it will serve as a reminder that they are not to pick up the old issue again. This commitment is the foundation of new pleasant relationships; but, most of all, it is the framework for inner freedom and peace in your heart, knowing that there is nothing left for Satan to use as an accusation against you. God has forgiven and removed all guilt. "There is therefore now *no* condemnation for those who are in Christ Jesus" (Romans 8:1). Thank God for His marvelous design in giving us the capacity to forgive and be forgiven!

Responsibility plus *release* equals *rehabilitation.* The responsibility of acknowledging our sin and the release of forgiveness by Christ and others results in the rehabilitated heart and mind that are at peace with self, God, and others.

> "Let *the peace of Christ* rule *in your hearts. . . . and be thankful*" (Colossians 3:15).

How exciting to be a personal friend
of the One who knows who I really am,
what I feel inwardly, what I shall ultimately
accomplish, and where I shall go from here.

5

Step Out With Confidence

Have you ever considered the fantastic process we call memory? The mind is a powerful data processing center that throughout our life receives and recycles information, experiences, and emotional impressions. There is strong scientific evidence that even a ten-day-old baby records and retains memories of events. What a tremendous impact this has on our future! There are happy, delightful memories stored to cheer us when we are lonely. When winter clouds gather and the snow covers the garden, we remember the beauty of sunshine and springtime flowers. A grandmother in a rest home finds her long day brightened by the memory of a child's laughter.

The logical order of memory playback is marvelous, too. Wouldn't it be terrifying if suddenly we were bombarded with all of our memories at exactly the same moment? Instead, the ability to recall is triggered by similar or related stimuli that remind us of past experiences.

If this amazing ability is misused, it becomes one of the most destructive forces in the world, for the same faculty that records and retains memories of beauty, love, and happiness also retains imprints of hate, injustice, poverty, suffering (though we cannot recall the feeling of pain), fear, and all of humanity's ills. Why, then, do we not recognize that we must discipline the way we use this power?

By nature, all people are selfish or self-centered. We hang on to things such as cars, houses, nice clothes, membership in organizations, and influential acquaintances as evidence to ourselves that we are safe. We hope these will assure us of acceptance by others. But inwardly we long to be valued and wanted as a person.

We record the impression we feel we have made on others, whether it is good or bad. A friend may tell me I am generous. I find myself wanting to do something nice for her. Another may cause me to feel clumsy or inferior, and I react by stumbling or dropping things when I am with her.

Several years ago, I spent each Tuesday falling over cartons, dropping books, and bumping into counters. Why? That was the day I left my familiar ground as a consultant on educational materials to work in a foreign world of literature. Christie, a lovely, dynamic woman with an inexhaustable knowledge of authors and books, owned the store. Just to be near her produced an instant reaction of having ten thumbs and six feet. The expertise of another, if measured against my limitation, can paralyze normal performance and future relationships and activities. The memory of their image of me (as I believe it to be) becomes the focus of my attention for the moment and it influences my actions.

The more secure a person is in the love and respect of family and friends, the less importance is attached to those impressions. It was a very special day when Christie shared with me needs in her personal life. As we prayed together, I realized that she was not an untouchable paragon of knowledge, but a dear wife and mother just like myself. I did not need to compete to prove myself infallible or perfect. I was free to be myself, for I was loved and respected regardless of imperfection. It was no longer performance or possessions, but myself as a person who was valued. This is the image factor that causes us to behave differently with different people. A critical person finds others reacting with tension and defensiveness. A warm, happy person generates a relaxed atmosphere without pressure. There is no longer the danger of being attacked verbally.

Reactions are fed by memories of past experiences. When I was five years old, I ate too much coconut cream pie and became ill. Today I seldom eat it and never by choice. That experience forty years ago has programmed my reactions today. We have a built-in defensive action that attempts to protect us from future hurt based on past experience via memory. We say to one who has hurt us, "I forgive you," but inwardly we add, "I cannot forget."

There is a strong tendency today to excuse our hang-ups because of childhood experiences or seeming parental failure. Actually, each of us is responsible for the way in which we react to any experience. I have a friend who is an outstanding Christian coach and educator. His father was an alcoholic; his brother is also. The two sons grew up in the same environment. One programmed his mind with the failure of his father and condemned him. It became such a focal point of his attention that he became what his dad had been. The other son said, "My father had a great need. I will build the best life possible, under God, that I may help him."

Memory became motivation to one and destruction to the other. One gave forgiveness and the other resentment and self-pity. Each was responsible for his reaction to the situation and his attitude toward it. Escapism and blame reproduced that which was most despised, while responsibility and honesty became the foundation of a life given to help others.

Proverbs 23:7 tells us that, "As he (a man) thinketh in his heart, so is he" *(King James Version)*. Our thought patterns are recorded in the sound track of the mind, and future contacts and experiences will trigger the mechanism of the brain to play back those impressions. Each time we play back any thought, the recording groove becomes deeper. Eventually the groove has become so well-established that we find ourselves unable to "play" a new tune.

God has given us a marvelous blueprint for training our thought processes. In Philippians 4:6-9 we read, "Don't worry over anything whatever; tell God every detail of your needs in earnest and thankful prayer, and the peace of God, which transcends human understanding, will keep constant guard over your hearts and minds as they rest in Christ Jesus. Here is a last piece of advice. If you believe in goodness and if you value the approval of God, *fix your minds* on whatever is true and honourable and just and pure and lovely and praiseworthy. Model your conduct on what you have learned from me, on what I have told you and shown you, and you will find that the peace of God will be with you" *(Phillips)*. We are told to "fix our minds," that is, *focus* our attention without permitting it to stray. Lock in the thoughts on this channel, pattern, or blueprint.

We are to deliberately exert effort and think about the things we know to be true, pure, lovely, and praiseworthy rather than the critical analysis of determining what is wrong with everybody else. Those positive character traits listed in Philippians

4 are the characteristics of God Himself. Thus, the Spirit of God will work in our minds and hearts to conform and transform us so that we may truly be a personality "in the image of God." Remember, "As (a man) thinketh in his heart, so is he." We are to think about God's character so that He may produce in us the result of that thought process which is to bear His family resemblance. We then become "look-alikes" with Jesus Christ, in spite of all our imperfections, and people can see God living in the world today through our lives. The more we focus our attention upon this pattern, the deeper the image or likeness becomes.

Confidence From Positive Thoughts

It is the natural reaction of many people to think negatively of themselves and others and to expect dire results from every experience. If you are one of the millions who have specialized in recording negative sound tracks, there is a marvelous experience available to you. You can cut a new "tape." I cannot change my thought processes by condemning myself because they are wrong. By so doing, I am only building a new negative focus. But if I begin taping over materials that have already been recorded, I will find that as the new recording is made, the first one is erased.

Man has a conscience or an awareness of guilt that demands forgiveness and cleansing. It is this capacity that motivates a person to correct attitudes and actions. It is only when we refuse to face the guilts and ignore or deny them that we become ill. For it is then that we have rejected, either intentionally or unknowingly, the very purpose for which we have that awareness of need.

But often memories may return. If I have thought these things so many times for so many years, they are apt to "bleed through" or, in the right set of circumstances, trigger the memory bank, and I am reminded of them. How marvelous then is God's promise that as I recognize their existence, I can relinquish them into His hands. There is a discipline of determining to think God's thoughts as He has commanded us to do in establishing our new "sound system."

As we think of cutting a new record successfully, there are certain things that are important. A dirty recording head will distort sound in a quality recording. The higher quality the production, the more important is the cleanliness of the equipment. Even the tiniest particles of dust and lint can become magnified, spoiling the end result. You may be sure that the greater the purpose God has for your life, the deeper will be the cleansing.

Our thoughts today program our actions of the future. Therefore, we must program our minds with real care. The "dust" of self-pity can become magnified to produce resentment and bitterness that is disastrous. There is also danger from the "lint" of critical analysis. The ability to recognize the faults and mistakes of others should lead us to realize that all of their shortcomings are simply cries for help. They are the visible display of inward, unseen needs. If we have that marvelous insight to recognize the needs of others, then it becomes our responsibility to pray for them lest we become judges of those whom God loves and for whom Jesus Christ died. If God does not condemn them, how dare we do so?

Debbie found that the challenge to become a peacemaker was a call to spiritual maturity. As a young pastor's wife, she soon learned the difficulty of finding a time when she and Jim could be alone. Cheri was the most persistent invader of those prized moments. Whenever Jim's car touched the driveway, Cheri was sure to follow. Dressed in hot pants at breakfast, a mini skirt at lunch, and a sizzler at dinner, she would appear with her latest assortment of problems that required immediate pastoral counsel.

Finally, in desperation, Debbie set her alarm ten minutes earlier than usual so she might pray for a solution. At first, she asked God to prevent the constant visits and interruptions. But soon she began praying that she might understand the needs that would motivate such a continual demand for attention.

One day she learned that Cheri's father had been a traveling evangelist with little time to hear a child's daily chatter. Understanding was the beginning of healing. Debbie and her husband cooperated in shifting the time spent in counseling to developing friendship between the two women. Soon they launched a Listening Post Bible Club for children of working or absentee parents. Cheri did not find instant release from a lifetime of longing for a concerned, spiritual authority figure, but in working with children who had similar needs, she began recognizing behavior problems in her life and began coping with them on a responsible, adult level.

Life in the parsonage is not a sudden utopia for Debbie. There will be a continuing procession of people and problems. But through this experience, a barrier has become a bond between herself and her husband. Her personality is lovelier and her ministry richer as resentment and criticism have given way to confidence and understanding.

It is absolutely impossible to be truly happy and still be critical and condemning of others at the same time. Isn't it wonderful that Jesus Christ, while enduring the unspeakable agony of Calvary, did not judge others? He said, "Forgive those who have done this to me" (Luke 23:34). He has given us forgiveness, and now we must pass it on to those who need our forgiveness. It is a treasure that expands with every use! The more we give, the more we are able to receive, for our capacity is increased.

After the "dust" and "lint" have been cleared away, you are ready to begin the process of building new thought patterns for health and happiness. The secret of programming our minds and memory banks lies in three steps of communication.

Ask
Thank
Praise

Many, many times God invites, encourages, and commands us to *ask* Him for whatever we need. Then why are we so hesitant to do so? Is it because we have a vague, factual theory that God will answer but not an actual expectancy of seeing anything tangible happen? Is it that we have so spiritualized the truths of the Bible that we do not see the concrete reality of the power of God in our everyday living? Is it that we are afraid of being disappointed simply because our concept of God is unreal? Do we think of Him as remote and concerned only with matters of vast importance?

The truth is that the moment you receive Jesus Christ as your Savior, the spirit of God is living within your body. He inhabits your being! Everything that happens to you happens to Him. Certainly He is concerned in every detail, for He is a part of all things. Ask Him for everything that is good and right, but leave the final decision to Him as to whether it is best to give or withhold or perhaps postpone your request for the moment. Allow Him the freedom to choose the time in which He will answer and in the way He knows is best. All that He gives or withholds is for your good because He loves you.

Secondly, we are told to "thank God at all times for everything" (Ephesians 5:20,(*Phillips)*. If he gives or withholds for my good, certainly I should *thank* Him for the loving wisdom of His decision for my well-being. Only He knows what will happen tomorrow, next month, or next year. That which seems, from my limited viewpoint, the only answer to my need or happiness may be overruled by His knowledge of the end result.

Are you thinking today, "I do not feel thankful for this situation that I am facing"? That's all right. He does not say that we must "feel thankful." To give thanks does not depend upon our feelings, but upon His command. We are simply told to do it. If you had a serious heart condition and your doctor prescribed a strict diet, would it be hypocritical to follow that diet if you did not "feel" like it? Nonsense! You long for health and healing, and you would follow the guidelines that an expert in your field of need had given you. Feelings and emotions are flighty and change with the color of the sky. With the return of health you will "feel" differently.

Your feelings are not to control you, but rather you are to control them. And it is far more true in the spiritual realm than in the physical. The Great Physician has rightly diagnosed our heart trouble and has given us the diet of thanksgiving and praise. It will change the focus of our attention from the problem to the God who is over the problem. Feelings will change, for they are the result of attitude and action. We long for peace and joy, and both flow from a believing mind and heart.

The third step is the beginning of a marvelous

adventure in *praise*. God has told us that we are to praise Him. It is mentioned literally hundreds of times in the Bible. If it has occupied so much of our Father's attention, then it must have some amazing importance in our lives. We thank God for what He *does*, but we praise Him for what He *is*. When we praise Him, we discover what He is really like. He has told us that we are created "for the praise of His glory!"

Praise, a Key to Confidence

There can be no lasting happiness until we begin to fulfill the purpose for which God has designed us. It is absolutely impossible to worry, fear, or be depressed when we look at His character and sing the love song of praise to His glory. A child who is worried about bread for dinner does not reflect confidence in his parents' love or ability to provide. Praise is simply the child of God gathering up all of his limitations, fears, and worries and finding them swallowed up in the greatness of God.

As you begin to explore the delights of praise, some incident may occur to tempt you to relive unpleasant memories. Perhaps this is an important checkpoint at which you may reach out for new growth. It is a time of driving down a stake and mounting a flag of victory, of reminding yourself that this area of life has been given to God — it is no longer yours. It is a time of enlarging your communications with God in asking and receiving the results of healing prayer, emotionally and spiritually. It is a reminder, if you are still inclined to resent or criticize others, that you are obligated to pray for them and to show love to them. Knowledge brings responsibility. Could this be your very special service of love to God — your home mission field — to pray daily for the needs of those in your home? While they may not show an immediate sense of appreciation or change, God will reward you, for your service is unto Him. You will discover that in the process walls between you and others will have crumbled and resentments disappeared.

As you pray and praise, program your thoughts with precious promise verses. Use the wasted times of day and night, those minutes while waiting on a bus, at a traffic light, or while showering and doing the many mechanical activities that do not require your thought, to store up rich treasures of God's promises to you. Choose verses that meet specific needs in your life and memorize them. How rich the investment of time and interest will become as you cooperate with the Spirit of God in giving Him the storehouse of memory so that you may draw upon it in future needs.

If there is anything that Satan does not want to have happen in your life, it is these three things:

1) He does not want your life to be to the praise of God's glory, for it makes you beautiful. It smooths out worry lines and brightens your personality with a fresh sparkle. It insures you

of all the happiness that God has designed and created you to achieve.

2) He does not want you to be in constant touch with God's control center through prayer, for it makes you calm and powerful. You become invulnerable to Satan's power through Christ.
3) He does not want you to be armed with the Word of God, which is the Sword of the Spirit, for it will ultimately, totally defeat him.

The warfare is between God and Satan, and you have declared yourself to be of value to one team or the other by the position you take toward people, places, and circumstances. How wonderful that Jesus Christ saves us eternally from Satan and sin, but He saves you now from the conflict created by sin that is always destructive. Its taproots are doubt and pride. These, in turn, produce the worry, guilt, and fear that we experience. Confident resting in the arms of Jesus Christ, relaxing in the knowledge of His love and provision, produces faith.

What is faith? Listen to these words of Hebrews 11:1-3: "Now faith means putting our *full confidence* in the things we hope for, it means being certain of things we cannot see. It was this kind of faith that won their reputation for the saints of old. And it is after all only by faith that our minds accept as fact that the whole scheme of time and space was created by God's command — that the world which we see has come into being through principles which are invisible" (*Phillips*).

Faith is setting aside our limitations to lean hard on an unlimited God. It is to depend upon His character of love, faithfulness, wisdom, and power rather than on the unlovely things I am aware of in my own personality which is still in the process of being remodeled. This faith is the total basis for my confidence and the assurance that my life is being guided, guarded, and controlled as I pass through the many changes that are necessary.

I can have strong confidence in myself as a person for God has a reason for my existence. My confidence is not limited to one person standing alone, for it rests on a majority of two: God and I together. Positively *nothing* can happen today that God and I can't handle together! What a tremendous motivation to see myself and others from God's point of view!

Each precious moment of this day — this very hour in fact — is a gift of God that will never return again. It is yours to invest for the future as you intelligently present your mind to Jesus Christ and experience the fulfillment of Philippians 2:3-4: "Live together in harmony, live together in love, as though you had only one mind and one spirit between you. Never act from motives of rivalry or personal vanity, but in humility think more of each other than you do of yourselves. None of you should think only of his own affairs, but should learn to see things from other people's point of view" (*Phillips)*.

"Let this mind be in you, which was also in Christ Jesus" *(King James Version)*. The mind of Christ is your pattern and goal. Confidence under God's control can become the norm of your daily life as you deliberately develop the discipline of memory and thoughts. "Forgetting those things which are behind, and reaching forth unto those things which are before" (Philippians 3:13, *King James Version*). Reaching forth to a future controlled by the promises of God!

> *"Being confident of this very thing, that he which hath begun a good work in you* will *perform it until the day of Jesus Christ"* (Philippians 1:6, *King James Version).*

The love of God can be seen most clearly in the display case of daily living.

6
Step Into the Adventure of Love

My whole world seemed to be falling apart. Never had I felt so deserted, so lonely. Why should I love others who continually hurt me?

"Certainly I love God, but. . . ."

"June, there are no buts with God!" Doctor Bob's voice was gentle as he began unfolding the need of every human heart for unqualified love.

How often I have said, "I love my husband, my children, my friends, but. . . "Love is not a conditional exchange of favors." I will love you if you are kind to me, if you are considerate and make me feel as I would like to feel."

What is love? Certainly it is more than body chemistry, more than respect and admiration for character traits, abilities, and achievements. God does not command us to *like* one another but to *love* one another. I do not have to like other persons who may seem irritating, disagreeable, and thoroughly unpleasant. Like has to do with the response of one personality to another. It originates in the soul (mind, will, intellect, emotions). But I can and should love that unlikeable person, for love originates in the spirit. As my spirit aligns with the Spirit of God, I can look at others from His point of view and value them because He has made them and values them. It is to become objective instead of personalizing the attitudes and actions of others toward self. Their most unlovely characteristics are simply inward needs coming to the surface. It is their cry for help. It is the insecure who criticize others, for they dare not risk having their own opinions or plans challenged by difference in others.

The most selfish, demanding, abusive person in your life may be the one with the greatest need for love. You might be the person, chosen by God, who, by your attitude toward them, will become the beautiful display of the reality of God's love to them. Love is not an agreement with or approval of what they are doing or saying but simply a valuing of them as a person whom God values because He has given them life and has a definite purpose for it. It is likely that they as yet do not know God or His love.

Roberta is an amazing mother of two daughters who are radically opposite in personality and activities. Carol was a lovely, gentle, unselfish girl whom any mother would adore, whereas Mavis had a stormy disposition which moved from the tantrums of childhood to the traumas of adolescence. Belligerent, abusive rebellion, alcohol, and drugs left their mark. But the same daily, loving prayer and flow of gifts and cards followed both girls — one in Bible college and the other in a commune.

During those years of heartache and disappointment, Roberta prayed, "Dear Father, my tears cannot match Yours. The agony I feel for my child is so small compared to that which You felt for Your Son. I cannot bear to see the ugliness of sin that covers her life. But You could not look upon the sin which Jesus bore for me and for Mavis. Your Son was dead and yet He arose again and He lives. My child is dead in sin, but You will bring her new life, and she will live too. Dear God, are You showing me that the greatest thing I can do is to be consistent so she may see Your love for her through me? Then help me to reveal it clearly as You did on Calvary."

Today, both girls are married to Christian men and both are being used of God. Carol's gentle temperament is valuable to her as a missionary to children. Mavis and her husband utilize their background to accentuate the story of God's unchanging love and forgiveness as they work among college students. Gentle Carol would find it difficult to work among campus rebellions, while Mavis would be poorly suited to communicate quietly, gently to small children. The wisdom of God is equalled by His patience as He looks beyond this moment, this experience, and uses the magnetic power of His love, revealed through others, to draw us to Himself.

Love is communicated through the unconditional extending of undeserved kindness and respect for the worth of another. This worth has its origin in a common Creator, not in individual performance. It is based on respect for the intelligence and ability of God to accomplish His plan in a life in spite of the lack of visible evidence in the tiny segment of a life that we may see at this moment.

The love of which God speaks is not an emotion. It is a series of actions or behavior patterns, a shift of attitudes, that will eventually produce the feeling of love. Feelings flow from the combination of attitudes and actions as surely as water flows from a bubbling spring. How often wives have said to me, "I want to get a divorce because I do not love my husband any more, and he doesn't love me." They simply mean, "I do not *feel* love." For if we do not show love by actions and attitudes, we will not feel love.

"We know, and to some extent realize, the love of God for us because Christ *expressed it in laying down his life for us*. . . . let us love not merely in theory or in words — let us love in sincerity and in practice. . . . To us, the greatest demonstration of God's love for us has been his sending his only Son into the world to give us life through Him. We *see* real love, not in the fact that we loved God, but that he loved us and sent his Son to make personal atonement for our sins. If God loved us as much as that, surely we, in our turn, should love each other! . . . if we love each other God does actually live within us, and his love grows in us towards perfection. . . . for we realize that our life in this world is actually his life lived in us" (1 John 3:16, 18; 4:9-12, 17, *Phillips*).

Jesus Christ not only saves us from the penalty of sin through His holiness, death, and resurrection, but He saves us from the continuing power of sin by His Presence and Life within us. He is the pattern for our life relationships with one another. Sometimes I long for the end result of being like Him without the daily discipline of doing to and for others as He has done for me. Then it is good for me to look back and remember just what God has done for me. How big are the things that He has forgiven? How many times has He shown love to me when I was most undeserving? Who can I show this kind of love to today?

To show love to others is not an option for the Christian. It is a command. "You shall love your neighbor as yourself" (Matthew 22:39). We could rephrase it to read, "You must be willing to do anything that is of positive value for someone else that you would do for your own benefit." People marveled constantly at the love that Jesus showed *by His actions* to the most undeserving, lowest, unattractive people. It was to the inward, continuing person that He ministered, but it was through their outward, physical self. He didn't have to touch a leprous body. He could have just spoken and given healing. But He knew that those who had been called "unclean untouchables" needed to feel love and restoration in the touch of a caring hand.

It is that same hand that touches our lives today in meeting external and internal needs. The recognition of this love brings healing of many emotional disturbances. We read in 1 John 4:18, "There is no fear in love, but perfect love casts out fear. For fear has to do with punishment . . .". In 2 Timothy we discover that God has not given us the spirit of fear, but of power, love, and a sound mind. Certainly for the person who has never accepted the love of God through the forgiveness of sin there is fear of judgment after death as well as a fearful approach to the issues of life, but there is also an attitude of fear in the hearts and minds of God's people today. It is a fear that finds its basis in concentration on the turbulence of circumstances about them, failing health, loss of jobs, income, family, and possessions. It is often a fear of past failures, but it may be fear from a different source.

The Bible teaches us that "Satan is the accuser of the brethren"; it is his purpose to negate the absolute promises of God to His child.

There have been two images painted of your life, and you have bought one or the other! God has painted one of you as being His treasure, His custom-made creation whom He loves dearly — one with whom He shares thrilling adventures daily. But the debilitating, depressive, condemning attacks of Satan would suggest that you are an unloved, unappreciated failure, at least to some degree. Which image did you buy today?

You are the showcase of God's love so that your family and others may *see* a living, loving God through you. In order that you may remain transparent, the windows of your life need daily cleaning and polishing. Then you can radiate love, encouragement, and understanding so needed by your family and friends.

How many times we miss the opportunity to bring the healing of Christ's love to those who need it most. How often we are tempted to think, "If God will change my husband's (or child's) attitude or actions, then I can show love." "If I had a larger house (better income, newer car, or the removal of certain pressures), I could be more loving and kind." Actually, if our obedience to God's command is contingent upon God or an individual doing something that we feel should be done for us, it is *our attitude* that needs to be changed.

A gift is not a gift as long as we expect something in return. It is an exchange that we hope will result in our personal gain! A gift is an unconditional relinquishment to another of that which belongs to us so that we may give happiness or something of value, without hope of receiving anything in return. Often the barrier to happiness lies in the unwillingness to sacrifice a personal view as a love-gift to Christ. It is the bar across the door that prevents us from entering into the abundant life of peace and joy, of loving and being loved.

This fact is shown vividly in the story of a woman who came one day to share her needs.

She said, "I love my husband, but I am *not* going to pick up his clothes off the bathroom floor. He is just as capable of doing it as I am. He's nothing but a big, spoiled boy, and I refuse to humor him."

Later in our conversation she asked, "What am I going to do? Now he has left home, and I cannot pay the house payment or the bills. I just feel nauseated. What's going to happen to me?"

A few days later there was an opportunity to talk with her husband. He said, "I don't understand her. What does she expect from me? The day I left was too much. I walked in and asked for a cup of coffee (dinner is never ready and I'm hungry when I get home). But she yelled, 'Get it yourself,' while she sat in the easy chair. Then she asked me to go to the store and get some lettuce for a salad. I said, 'Get it yourself. You've had all day to go three blocks to the store and to cook a decent meal.' "

The real desire of this woman's heart was to have her husband show love and attention. She felt that he had been away all day in a swirl of people and interesting activities while she sat at home. Was she not entitled to more than just the back view of a head bent over a newspaper or television program each evening and a pile of discarded clothes in the morning? To him there was no glamor in a nine or ten-hour job filled with competitive pressures. It was important to him to have a few minutes to unwind with a cup of coffee and the news and to be met by a happy wife and the aroma of a well-planned meal. Each expected the other to show love, but neither set aside the personal desires to be loved in the way they were able to receive love. If we are to love others, it must be in a way they can understand and are capable of receiving.

Love Comes in Many Ways

Several years ago, a friend of mine was given a vacation trip to the East Coast to visit her family. While she was away, her husband had the entire house painted and carpeted, with some remodeling. It was to have been a special surprise to show his love for her. When she returned and saw the results, she became very angry. She said, "He just sent me home to get rid of me while he fixed the house the way he wanted it!" This man had expressed his love by doing something special for his wife rather than by verbalizing it, and she had insensitively missed it. How we need sensitive hearts that respond to love in whatever way it is given!

Many times our children attempt to show love in ways that we just are not perceptive enough to recognize. One day our five-year-old Jeff came to help me in the kitchen. We were expecting dinner guests. The floors were waxed and shining, and a special meal was under way. Jeff, anticipating my need for sugar in making desert, reached for the canister only to knock it onto the floor. He tried to scoop it up, and, in reaching for a bag to put it in, knocked the cream off the counter.

"Honey, just go out of the kitchen and let me clean it up!" I said sharply.

A minute later the Lord spoke to my heart, and I slipped into his room. There he sat at his little table, his chin on his chest, looking as if he had lost his last friend. He was just crushed, for in trying to show his love by "helping" mom, everything had gone wrong. He felt a complete failure. Seldom has my heart gone out to a child as it did to that little guy that day. I put my arms around him and asked him to come back and help me, for I needed him. Our guests did not need shining floors or elegant desserts. They needed to be in the atmosphere of a family who loved one another and could love them.

If we are to give away the love of God to others who have such desperate needs, it must begin at home. There is marvelous healing power in loving and being loved. It is not in the perfection of performance or faultless dialogue. It is in the valuing of one another, of learning the empathy that enables us to see things from one another's point of view — almost as if we had slipped inside their skin. It is in the setting aside of the desire to have others perform in a certain way toward us, to have our needs met first. It is to initiate acts of love without expecting anything in return, simply giving kindness untinged by selfishness.

Love must give or die. God is love, though love is not God. True love rests in the fact of Jesus Christ inhabiting our human body and living His life out through us. It originates with Him, and we are His channel through which it is made visible.

"Anyone who wants to follow me must put aside his own desires and conveniences and carry his cross with him every day and *keep close to me!* Whoever loses his life for my sake will save it, but whoever insists on keeping his life will lose it; and what profit is there in gaining the whole world when it means forfeiting one's self?" (Luke 9:23-25, *Living Bible*).

The word "life" in the Greek, in which the New Testament was originally written, is *psuche.* It is from this word that we get various words such as "psyche" or "soul." It is a word that includes the personality, the intellect, the will, and the emotions. Our thought processes and attitudes are a part of the psyche or soul. If we should transliterate this verse loosely, it would read, "If any person clutches tenaciously or hangs on to his own rights, attitudes, thought patterns, and selfish desires, he will destroy his soul or personality, intellect, emotions, and will."

That person will become a slave to her lower nature. Life will become an ever-decreasing circle of self-centered interest. She will become less and less concerned with or interested in others and more absorbed in her own thoughts and desires until they alienate her from others. Selfishness will cut her off from the very ones she desperately needs. When relationships with anyone in the family circle are broken, the family unit becomes weaker, even as a chain becomes shorter and weaker when links are removed. Lives are living links that affect one another deeply.

We may refuse to see or solve issues in relationships, but we are never mentally or emotionally free from them until forgiveness is given and received. Therefore, Jesus points out that a person may gain the whole world of material possessions, but if she has destroyed herself in the process, what has she really gained? She has become a loser of personal happiness and a castaway.

In thinking of a castaway, we think of loneliness. Loneliness can be a great asset. It is the indication of a need to enjoy the fellowship of Jesus Christ and other people. But self-inflicted loneliness which isolates us from God and one another is destructive. It is a loneliness that feeds on self-pity, bitterness, and resentment. This type of loneliness blames others for their lack of attention.

Jesus gives us the solution in this verse: "Whoever loses (turns loose of) his life for my sake will save it" (Luke 9:24). To relinquish our rights and our expectations of others, our desires and attitudes, our very thought processes for the sake of pleasing Christ and to give them as our love-gift into His hands will be the beginning of discovering that which He has been waiting and longing to give us. It is the emptying process that must come before He can do the filling.

We saw this illustrated one day as our two small sons came in from the beach. They were proud of their treasure from the sea as they showed us several small crabs in a carton of salt water. A few minutes later they asked if they could have some lemonade. When I went into the kitchen, I saw our lemonade pitcher on the counter, and in it were those ugly little crabs — salt water and all! Before it could ever be used to contain refreshing drink, the pitcher had to be emptied and cleaned.

Our lives become filled with the "brine" of daily experiences that must be emptied and cleansed. After the cleansing, we can receive the filling of the refreshing love of God — so much love that we cannot possibly contain it all. It must spill over into the lives of those within our home and total circle of influence.

Becoming "Look-Alikes"

In Luke 9:23 we are told to put aside our own desires and *follow* Jesus. The word "follow" in the Greek has such a beautiful meaning that it would take many English words to fully express it. The word connotes one who walks closely beside another and bears his resemblance. That is, by walking so closely they have become "look-alikes." When children are born into a family, there are certain resemblances which cause people to identify them as belonging to the same family. As they grow and develop, they show many of the attitudes and mannerisms of that home.

This is exactly what God is doing in our lives. He is developing His family likeness so that people who meet His children will recognize their resemblance to Jesus Christ. He does not spoil us by giving us what we want, but He gives us what we need. He shows His love the way He knows we can receive it and by respecting the right of each person to be an individual. He would have us show love to others in the same way — totally free of any conditional demands or expectations.

Several years ago a well-known doctor told me that no one becomes her best and highest self until she is secure in love. Certain surface changes may occur to gain temporary advantages or for self-preservation, but it is being loved as a person that releases the fountain of the soul to love in return — not because it is required or expected, but because that life has become secure and enriched through having received love.

As we do the possible, God delights in doing the impossible! He shares in abundance His love and life with you. Then you have an unlimited supply to give to all He brings your way, and your life is enriched in the process. He will not exhaust your resources without replenishing them far beyond your wildest dreams. The price of shining is burning, but it is the hand of God which provides both the match, the wick, and the oil for His lamp. Let your love-light shine without charge!

> "*We love him because he* first *loved us. . . . and . . . it is his explicit command that the one who loves God must love his brother too*" (1 John 4:19, 21, *Phillips*).

"To give unto them beauty for ashes,
the oil of joy for mourning,
the garment of praise
for the spirit of heaviness . . ."
(Isaiah 61:3, *King James Version*).

7

The Step of Power

"If I could just pull the covers over my head and forget there's a world out there to be faced. I'm too tired to tackle another day. . . ." Chris' voice trailed away.

She is one of many Americans who are afflicted with a disease that could be called "The Exhaustion Syndrome." Millions of people are weary and do not know why or the solution. But there are reasons and practical steps that can be taken to turn inertia into energy.

Hidden beneath the blanket of fatigue there is a new you waiting to be revealed. A lovelier you, who stands tall and breathes deep of the provisions for every need. A you who walks lightly by faith, in confidence and kindness, in praise and in power when the blanket that traps and binds is removed.

Spiritual Exhaustion

Fatigue can stem from organic reasons, but in most cases it has an entirely different basis. Too often even the organic problems are a result of other conditions. Physical, emotional, or psychological exhaustion are very real, but there is a deeper weariness than any of these. It is spiritual exhaustion. The spirit becomes weary when it is not properly connected to the source of all energy and power — God Himself. Weariness is basically the absence or misuse of power.

There is a straight, simple line to the release of power that originates in the heart and mind of God. Jesus said, "All power is given unto me" (Matthew 28:18, *King James Version)*, whether it is heaven or on earth, in eternity or in this era of time. And again we read, "In him (Jesus Christ) dwelleth all the fulness (power) of the Godhead bodily" (Colossians 2:9, *King James Version*). It is possible to desire the power of God in our life without recognizing that it is in Jesus

Christ, but we cannot take the gifts without the giver Himself, for they are *in Him.*

Today, I can walk in the warmth of the sunshine because a glowing ball, approximately 93,000,000 miles away in space, projects light, heat, and other rays essential to life. Without the sun, our earth would become a frozen planet of death. The sun *is* power. We long for peace, joy, freedom, power, security, hope, and happiness, but they are all wrapped up in the Person of Christ. If we are to have them, we must have Him. But how can we "have Him"?

Each person is unique, and Jesus comes to us in different ways. When I was five years old, Mrs. Williams, a neighbor, took me to Sunday school for three Sundays. The stories of Jesus and His love for children thrilled my heart. Then one day she decided that I should stay for church. I heard the pastor's voice thunder and his fist crash down upon the pulpit with a resounding thud, and I was terrified. I couldn't stop crying, and I was promptly escorted home. I had "misbehaved" in church and was not permitted to go back. I had to wait "until I was older."

As I watched Mrs. Williams' car drive away each Sunday, I would shut my eyes and visualize a circle of children hearing the stories of Jesus' love for little people. One day I saw other neighbors rushing into the Williams' home and soon was told that she had gone to be with Jesus. I cried because she had gone so far away to heaven and I did not know how to get there. I thought I would never again hear about Jesus.

My dear mother and dad were good, kind people, but there was almost no communication in our home. Dad was away most of the time and mom was locked up emotionally in her loneliness. Often during my early teen years my pillow was wet with tears — tears of longing for someone with whom I could talk, someone who understood the strange feelings of adolescence. The warm Tennessee summer breeze would touch my face and a wild emptiness seemed to shriek for something or someone. But I did not know what I wanted.

One day we moved to a different area. There a neighbor took me to an evangelistic crusade. The last night of those meetings I listened to the preacher expound the reality of heaven and hell and the need for a personal decision to receive Christ. I went forward with an overwhelming desire to know Him. Two ladies came to me and said, "We will pray for you." After they had prayer, they asked, "Now, do you know that you are a Christian?"

"I don't feel any different," I replied.

They said, "We will pray for you again." They prayed and, looking at me hopefully, they asked, "Now, do you know that you are a Christian?"

"I'm sorry," I said, "but I feel just the way I did when I came here."

They looked at me in dismay and one said to the other, "What awful sin keeps this child from God?" They turned away, and I found myself standing alone. Soon the neighbor who had brought me finished chatting with other women and took me home. That was the most miserable night of my life. The visiting evangelist was leaving the area immediately after the meeting and I did not know anyone who could tell me how I might find God. If my neighbor had known, wouldn't she have told me? If my parents knew, wouldn't they have taught me long ago?

The years that followed were a lengthy trail of searching for some intangible something. Perhaps I needed to find a nice fellow and have my own home. At eighteen I was married. Those were the years of World War II, and our lives revolved around the nightclub circuit. Chicago, Florida, Palm Springs, San Francisco, Las Vegas — from bright lights to brighter ones until the glare became the same. The blare of bands playing the same old beat. One night on the Vegas Strip, God began unwinding years of loneliness that no crowd could fill. Leaving the grand opening of the newest resort, I began walking toward the open desert. The stars were magnificent. I thought, "Strange that they never seem to collide with one another. Apparently, they have no problem in maintaining their own well-ordered orbit." If there was a God who could create such harmony and beauty, why would He not do as much for people? Why couldn't I find a worthwhile reason for living?

The next day we left for Oakland, California where we had decided to lease an apartment. We agreed that I would quit work and bring home our little boy who had been in private boarding homes or with grandparents most of his life. I had no idea what I would do with a five-year-old child, but I had seen a sign advertising "Vacation Bible School for All Boys and Girls." I had no idea what a Vacation Bible School was and even less idea about what to do with our son! But the sign had said "All Boys and Girls," so at least he was qualified. It seemed a happy solution. He would be there until noon each day. Naptime would fill the afternoon, then supper and bedtime. I would have two whole weeks to learn how to raise a child!

Monday morning found us squeezed into a line of wiggly, squealing children waiting to be enrolled. If there was anything I especially disliked, it was children! Yet here I was surrounded by a clamoring sea of them. I never dreamed that in a few short weeks I would begin working with children and that it would continue through the years to include thousands of youngsters. But there we were and there was God!

Activities soon began taking place at the far end of the room. I heard a fantastic story of Jesus Christ and watched it unfold in picture form on the flannelgraph board. Twenty years slipped away. Because of my little son, I had found God's Son again! A story told to five-year-olds picked up where a kindergarten teacher had left off long ago. Soon afterwards I went home almost dazed by the beauty of the story.

As I walked into the kitchen, my hand reached for

the timer on the stove. After setting it for thirty minutes, I said, "That story was beautiful. I really do not know who You are, Jesus, but if it is true that You are the Son of God and that You care about me, that You can stop the fury of a storm at sea, won't You stop the storms in my life?" I held up three fingers to an invisible God and continued, "I can't control these three problems in my life (and I named them one by one). Can you handle them for just thirty minutes?"

Thirty minutes later I set my timer for an additional half hour and discovered that God had taken care of all three for each period of time. Launching out in faith, I set the time for an hour and learned that God was adequate! Holding out my hands to empty space, I said, "I don't know anything about You or Your Bible, but I do know that You have just done what I could not do. Won't You take control of every minute of each day for the rest of my life? I want to know You and learn how to love You, but You will need to be very patient with me for I am so ignorant. Will You teach me all that I need to know?"

That was about twenty-five years ago. God has never failed to meet any need of my life as an individual or our needs as a family, although He has shocked us many times with the unusual ways in which He has met them.

He will fill your life with beauty as you relinquish the ashes of dead experiences, hurts, and fears. He *is* alive! But you can only see Him through believing that what He has said, He will do. For me, there were no bells ringing, no lights shining. It was simply taking God at His word. What a tremendous expansion of faith, freedom, and power God has available for us as we relinquish the control of our short-term physical existence to Him. How often weariness disappears as the reality of God's Word becomes operative: "*The joy of the Lord is your strength*" (Nehemiah 8:10). It is spiritual joy that conquers so many exhausting experiences.

Emotional Exhaustion

The experiences which sometimes seem the most wearying can become the most valuable to us. Gold is refined by heat, and the hotter the fires, the purer the finished product. "Who are kept by the power of God through faith unto salvation ready to be revealed in the last time. . . . That the trial of your faith, being much more precious than of gold that perisheth, though it be tried with fire, might be found unto praise and honour and glory at the appearing of Jesus Christ" (1 Peter 1:5, 7).

The hotter the fire, the greater the conflict, the greater our need, and the greater the end result which is the beautiful life fashioned by it. Kings' jewels require extra polishing, and God claims His children as His jewels! There is a golden you that shines all the brighter after the polishing of buffeting circumstances.

That's the way that I met Mrs. Johnson. We had

moved into a home near the beach, and our two small sons were skipping down the sidewalk. Suddenly, without warning, our new neighbor turned and directed a heavy stream of water from her hose on them, telling them to stay off of her sidewalk.

It was easier to wipe away their tears and give dry clothes than to still the feelings of retaliation in my own heart. "Love your enemies . . . pray for them which despitefully use you. . . ." The words of Jesus in Matthew 5:44 echoed in my mind.

"But, Lord, she is wrong and miserably unkind."

Like a gentle whisper, His Spirit prompted, "If she dislikes children so much, she must have been terribly hurt by them."

The next day I took a lovely Easter lily to her. I found that she was elderly and terribly lonely. Her flowers were her world. I soon learned that she had adult children who never came to see her even though they lived nearby. How deep had been her wounds as she spent Mother's Day, Christmas, and other days without seeing her grandchildren. After being rejected by them, she had rejected others who served as a sharp reminder of her pain.

We soon became friends, sharing plants and children. Who would have thought our Lord intended that we discover our new "stand-in" grandmother through hurt feelings that triggered an angry reaction?

Anger can be used to express wonderfully satisfying works of kindness and love. It can generate new energy and vitality rather than leaving one depressed, defeated, and weary. After all, who gained the most in my experience: neighbor, children, or myself? What a shame to cheat ourselves and others of happiness that God has planned for us.

Anger is misdirected energy, and is often a result of feeling hurt. Someone or something has violated our convictions, ethics, religious, political or social opinions. We are concerned with the daily trivia that represents our personal tastes, likes and dislikes, such as: money spent, the way the table is set, laundry done, food prepared, or a host of other things. We resent freedoms or privileges we believe others may have, especially if they seem to be had at our expense. We become angry and feel abused.

We simply must find a way to express anger in a positive way that will accomplish good, or we will push it down and cover it until the "lid blows." If we give others "a piece of our mind" too often, we may not have enough left for ourselves! Usually it is those who cause us to feel the greatest surge of anger who have the deepest needs for kindness. Certainly God is interested in getting us into heaven, but I am sure He is equally interested in getting a bit of heaven into our hearts and homes here and now.

Fear is another tremendous robber of dynamic energy. For Karen it was the fear of growing old, of losing admiration, companionship, respect, and approval of husband, children and friends. Her fears had become a cleverly disguised depressant. Unconsciously her attention was focused upon her outward appearance rather than on the inward spirit. Each new line, shadow, or wrinkle, each added pound or tinge of gray added to the growing insecurity. Her outward reaction became either a total abandonment of attention to personal grooming or an over-exaggeration in make-up, but the inward fear was the same.

Many of the most interesting, creative, respected, valued, sought-after people I know are wearing silver haloes. Their hair has long since lost the shades of youth, but the inner personality of kindness, patience, wisdom, understanding, forgiveness, gentleness, and hope are so winsome that it is a sheer delight to people of all ages to be with them. Personality, character, and faith only increase in richness with age.

It is when one depends upon the outward physical appearance to compensate for inward lack of beauty that there is reason to react to approaching age. If that is the case with you today, then change your emphasis! Begin developing the *inner* person who *never* deteriorates. It is only transplanted from earth to heaven! We are just a bit nearer to the reality of the new body that we shall receive from our Lord than we were a year ago! Let's get the person ready to fill it! Truly you can take nothing with you except that which you have given away!

Physical Exhaustion

There is a reward in caring for your physical body

without unduly pampering it. Adequate rest, good grooming, a balanced diet, and vitamins, if needed, are essential to physical health. But often our best efforts are scuttled. Most of us no longer get enough oxygen to burn off excess fats. Oxygen is a fuel or source of energy. We try to compensate for weariness by eating more food. Often the problem is only increased and so is our weight!

Much of the heavy physical work that was once a part of everyday living is now passé. As a result we simply do not breathe deeply. The intake of oxygen is limited, to say nothing of an exposure to polluted air! Even many of our heating systems take much of the oxygen from the air.

One gloomy Monday I felt as if each step was torture. I had to get through the details of lunch bags, breakfast, and school clothes. At last, with a hurried good-bye, the children were off, the house was quiet and still. I walked across the patio feeling too weary to care about the activities of the day. Stooping to enjoy the fragrance of a rose, I began pulling the stray weeds nearby. Soon I was busily at work with the rejuvenating freshness of sunshine and air all around me. A brisk walk or even a few deep breaths of air can awaken new energy as we take a fresh supply of oxygen into our depleted system.

Take a good look at yourself in the mirror. What do you see? When we let our body sag, we feel old. Good posture helps defeat fatigue. Take a deep breath. With your shoulders back and your tummy tucked in, you look and feel better. Stand tall and reach for the ceiling with your head. Your lungs can function much better, and there are many physical and psychological benefits of standing tall.

Remember the truths of our first chapter that we shared together? You *are* very special to God. Look yourself in the eye and say right out loud, "Dear God, thank You for making me. I am Your handiwork. Thank You for walking in my body today. I am happy to share it with You." Smile at yourself! If you won't, why expect anyone else to do so? The Bible does not offer crowns for frowns or trophies for mopeys! But it does tell us of the ministry of encouragement, hospitality, and friendliness and the delightful rewards that God gives.

Happiness Is . . .

The principles I have shared with you in this little book are God's rules to make happiness a reality in your life. Because they are God's laws they will achieve the purpose for which He has designed them in any life where they are operational. Many people enjoy the benefits of one or more of them without ever recognizing the God who gave them. For instance, there are those who have learned through life experiences that "As you sow, so shall you reap" (Galatians 6:7). That is, to give kindness, understanding, and encouragement to others enriches the life of the person who gives. This is a guideline that God has set in motion.

In the preface of this book I mentioned Kevin, a fourteen-year-old boy who lived in the agony of a home shattered by conflicts. He said, "My mother and dad are Christians. We go to church, pray, and tithe our income to God. But in our attitudes toward each other, it seems as if we are trying to prevent one another from being happy. You would think we hate each other. My best friend does not go to church. His parents are atheists, and yet they like one another. What is wrong with our family?"

There is no lack in the Bible nor is there any negligence on God's part to produce the beautiful life for which we long. He is the One who gives us that very longing. The simple fact is that while many Christian families have discovered the principle of God that brings forgiveness for the nature of sin — the salvation that opens the doors of heaven to them for eternity — they have ignored His other principles for our spiritual growth and health. They are secure in their relationship in the family of God and assured of the joy in His Presence throughout all the ages. But, in the meantime, while living on this earth, they will experience a continual process of God's schooling. Many of the painful and difficult happenings are designed or permitted by God that we may discover the tremendous release from the self-directed life and come into the marvelous freedom and joy of the Christ-directed life.

Kevin's friends had not yet discovered God's provision of salvation in Jesus Christ, and if they do not do so, in eternity there will be unending agony and separation from God. The years that have been given to them by the hand of their gracious Creator have been invested in short-term living: the self-centered interests of life on this earth with absolutely no preparation for eternity. But during this time they have discovered the harmony that results from setting aside personal rights and desires in order to show kindness to others. Because it is a truth of God, it will benefit the lives of those who use it, even though they do not recognize the God who authenticated it. Kevin has the privilege of sharing with them God's program for the future and gaining from their experience the practical challenge of showing kindness and forgiveness in his home.

The Christian certainly has more reason to develop these attitudes in daily living than others for he has acknowledged that they are from God. All too often increased understanding of the way in which we should respond to others results in an expectation or even a demand that others treat us this way while our attitude becomes critical or disdainful if they do not do so. How easy to recognize that "This is what's wrong with John. He sure needs to change," when in reality, it is we who need to change and have our life directed by those principles.

Kindness is not told; it is shown by life attitudes toward others. It must be put in operation in our lives *before* we can expect it to become operative in the lives of others. The Christian has the added resources of God to implement these guidelines. How can we expect more of those who are as yet without Christ, or who perhaps have just come to know Him, than we ourselves are showing through our attitudes and actions? It is not vast knowledge of scriptural truths that captivates the heart in desperate need. It is the life governed by God.

These are seven steps in God's governing love designed to give hope, freedom, peace, joy, full confidence, security, love, and power. It is my prayer for you that this will not be a closed book, but an open *life*, as you take a last look at these principles.

If we are to walk each day in the expectant hope that happiness will be ours in this life and in a far greater, unlimited, unmarred perfection eternally, we must remember the principle of uniqueness. The all-wise, ever-loving God knew what He was doing when He specifically custom-designed you for His glory. No one in this world can achieve that purpose as well as you can, nor will you be as happy as you could be if you do not have the confidence in Jesus Christ to guide you through His matchless purpose to fulfillment. The birth of hope swirls us high above the monotony of the masses as we recognize that we are God's unique creation. There will never be another you!

If you are searching for buoyant, unshackled freedom, it is to be found only as you are lifted above the circumstances to fly high with God! Look at the happenings, places, people, and circumstances from God's point of view. Thrill to the fact that His love designs the confrontations you face, for it is in this facing of conflicts that you are healed and set free from fear, anxiety, and frustration. It is in the knowing that "old things are passed away" (2 Corinthians 5:17) that you are renewed and encouraged to look beyond this moment to the future that will be enriched by this experience.

Are you longing for peace? Oh, the marvelous calm of beginning each new day with a clean record, carrying nothing over from yesterday or the past. Accept with joy this brand-new day fresh from the hand of God! Never before have you had the opportunities and experiences that are yours today, and never again will they return in exactly the same way. The soiled clothing of yesterday has been discarded along with old attitudes and emotional wounds. All of nature is constantly discarding the old growth to burst into beautiful new vitality and blossom, and so must we. The gloomy closets of guilt and failure will not plague today; but the glory of the risen Son sends the beams of His light as the dawn breaks and there is a new day to share with Him.

Does joyful confidence seem an evasive, unattainable dream? That dancing, irridescent bubble will not burst and disappear as the look of faith visualizes the presence of Jesus Christ walking each moment with you. The lenses of your faith will be directed by a definite act of the will to focus upon those things which are of virtue, praise, and good report — those things which are the character of God — that you might cooperate in His transformation of your life; for as your thoughts are, so will you become. Memory can be disciplined as it becomes a reminder to praise, pray, and preserve His promises in your mind and heart. Your performance reflects the happy confidence of simply enjoying your Lord and investing the strength that He has given.

The intangible but essential security which seems to elude you so often is fashioned by the nail-scarred palms of the hands that have taken the responsibility for you and hold you close to His heart of love. There you can relax in His arms. Nothing can touch or shatter the peace of your Father's security, for it cannot be taken from you. All other things in which you can trust will be removed or changed, but God is the same yesterday, today, and forever. He delights in doing the impossible as you become willing to do the possible and leave the rest to Him. The differences between husband and wife, parent and child, and all of life's personal relationships become the completing of one another as you discover the reality of God's headship over your life.

The deepest and richest of all human needs and experiences is that of loving and being loved in the way that God has designed. It is to value each other and respect the differences in one another, allowing the freedom to be led by God rather than imposed ideas. Hold in valid trust the emotions, thoughts, words, and actions of others without the compulsion to compromise your own personality to conform to that which is less than God's best. Accept others as valuable, without necessarily agreeing with their behavior. Recognize that to give and receive love is not a bargaining with God or man, not an exchange of favors, but a giving of kindness without thought of return — a giving of total personality to complete other persons. The emptying of self and abandonment of concern with having personal needs met becomes your capacity to give and receive love. Learn the power of love that cannot be tarnished by fear. To love is to walk as Jesus Christ walked, for He does so again through you.

Vitality, energy, and motivation will rise from the ashes of weariness, depression, and frustrated disinterest as anger becomes the positive fuel that transforms hurts to heavenly high spots of positive actions, bringing healing to giver and receiver. You can stand tall on the back of fear that has been put under foot as you climb these stepping stones edged with gold.

God gave us a fantastic world, but we have been rather poor custodians. The ashes of our civilization hang heavy in space. But when the "heavens shall pass away with a great noise, and the elements shall melt with fervent heat" (2 Peter 3:10), those ashes will hold no appeal to the child of God who will occupy throughout eternity "a new heaven and a new earth. . . . and God himself shall be with them, and be their God. And God shall wipe away all tears from their eyes; and there shall be no more death, neither sorrow, nor crying, neither shall there be any more pain: for the former things are passed away" (Revelation 21:1, 3-4, *King James Version*).

God has given His life to you along with seven beautiful guidelines which can recreate His character within you. It is the life free of all facade, limitation, and self-gratifying interest that powers you with high voltage energy. The only path of hope, freedom, confidence, peace, love, security, and power is traced across the pages of history by the footprints of Jesus Christ. Walking with God becomes a chain reaction adventure as His steps become your steps and His life becomes your life. The world will see once more that God is alive as He walks this day through you!

> "*Give unto them beauty for ashes . . . that they might be called trees of righteousness . . . that he might be glorified*" (Isaiah 61:3, *King James Version*).